Editor
Leasha Taggart

Assistant Editor
Gisela Lee

Editorial Manager
Karen J. Goldfluss, M.S. Ed.

Editor-n-Chief
Sharon Coan, M.S. Ed.

Illustrator
Blanca Apodaca

Cover Artist
Lesley Palmer

Art Coordinator
Denice Adorno

Creative Director
Elayne Roberts

Imaging
Ralph Olmedo, Jr.

Product Manager
Phil Garcia

Publishers
Rachelle Cracchiolo, M.S. Ed.
Mary Dupuy Smith, M.S. Ed.

Daily Skills Practice

Grades 1-2

Author

Mary Rosenberg

Teacher Created Materials, Inc.
6421 Industry Way
Westminster, CA 92683
www.teachercreated.com

©2000 Teacher Created Materials, Inc.
Reprinted, 2002
Made in U.S.A.
ISBN-1-57690-514-4

Table of Contents

Introduction

Daily Skills Practice: Grades 1-2 was designed to cover a wide range of skills and concepts typically introduced or reviewed during a school year. The practice pages provide a quick assessment of how a child is performing on a particular skill or with a specific concept. In addition, the activities in this book provide teachers, children, and parents with consistent, daily feedback on a child's academic progress.

How to Use the Practice Pages

In the Classroom

The daily skills pages are easily implemented in the classroom during whole-class instruction. Here are some suggestions for introducing and assigning the pages:

- Give each child a photocopy of the daily practice sheet you wish to use, or prepare a small packet consisting of six to ten practice sheets for each child. (**Note:** A blank skills practice form has been provided on page 4. To add your own lessons to this book, write activities on the form before reproducing the page.) Send the packets home every one to two weeks. Decide how you will review and assess the children's completed work and communicate this to both the children and the parents.

- If you wish to use some or all of the practice sheets for whole-class or group instruction, simply photocopy them onto overhead transparency sheets and use them throughout the year. The transparencies can be organized and stored for use the coming year.

At Home

The practice pages in this book make excellent reinforcement exercises at home. With over 200 daily practice pages from which to chose, a child is given the opportunity to review concepts and skills he or she already knows. For newly acquired skills, the pages provide reinforcement through practice. As pages are completed, parents and children can correct the exercises using the answer key on pages 207–240.

Practice Page Sections

Each practice page is divided into the following three sections:

Five-a-Day

Five–a-Day consists of five math problems. Generally, there are three math problems and two word problems. The Five-a-Day section covers basic addition and subtraction skills. These include money, skip counting, measuring, fact families, place value, and time.

Sentence-a-Day

Each day's sentence contains at least two mistakes; a capital letter is needed at the beginning of the sentence and the appropriate punctuation (period, question mark, or exclamation point) is needed at the end of the sentence. The Sentence-a-Day section also covers subject-verb agreement, capitalization of proper nouns, and correct pronoun usage. Read each sentence aloud and let the child know how many errors are in the sentence. Ask the child to state the error and how the error can be corrected. The child circles each error in the sentence and crosses out any words that are not needed. He or she then write the sentence correctly on the lines provided.

Language Arts Skills

Each day, one specific skill or concept is presented. This section is an effective way to quickly preview or review a skill or to introduce a new concept to the child. Among the skills covered in this section are color words, number words, months of the year, days of the week, abbreviations, compound words, plurals, alphabetical order, nouns, verbs, adjectives, labeling, and phonics (vowels, beginning and ending sounds, blends, digraphs). For more specific skills and a listing of pages on which they are found, see the Table of Contents.

Name

Practice

Five-a-Day:

Sentence-a-Day

Five-a-Day: Numbers to 10

Draw 1 heart.	Draw 2 cookies.	Draw 3 balloons.
Draw 4 happy faces.		Draw 5 circles.

Sentence-a-Day

i   like   bears

_____

- - - - - - - - - - - - - - - - - - -

About Me!

My first name is _____.

My last name is _____.

I am _____ years old.

Name

Practice 2

Five-a-Day: Numbers to 10

Draw 6 triangles.	Draw 7 squares.	Draw 8 rectangles.
Draw 9 diamonds.	Draw 10 circles.	

Sentence-a-Day

meiko likes brown bears

ABC's

Copy the letters of the alphabet.

A B C D E F G H I J

K L M N O P Q R S T

U V W X Y Z

Name

Practice 3

Five-a-Day: Numbers to 10

Circle the number.

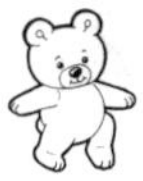

1 2

Circle the number.

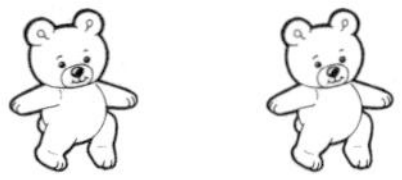

1 2

Circle the number.

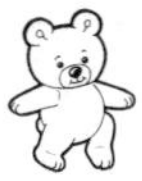

1 2

Circle the number.

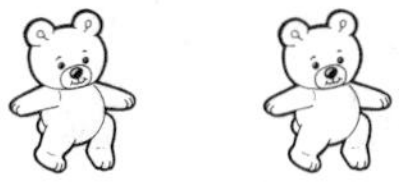

1 2

Circle the number.

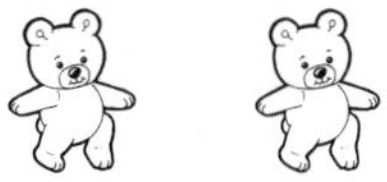

1 2

Sentence-a-Day

patty likes black bears

ABC's

Copy the letters of the alphabet.

a b c d e f g h i j

k l m n o p q r s t

u v w x y z

Five-a-Day: Numbers to 10

Write how many.	Write how many.	Write how many.
(bears) _____	(bears) _____	(bear) _____

Write how many.	Write how many.
(bear) _____	(bears) _____

Sentence-a-Day

julio   likes   honey   bears

_____

- - - - - - - - - - - - - - - - - - -

_____

ABC's

Write the missing letters of the alphabet.

A __ C __ E __ G __ I

J __ L M __ O __ Q R S T

U __ W X __ Z

Five-a-Day: Numbers to 10

Circle the number.	Circle the number.	Circle the number.
3 4	3 4	3 4

Circle the number.	Circle the number.
3 4	3 4

Sentence-a-Day

lucy   likes   bears,   too

ABC's
Write the missing letters of the alphabet.

a b ___ d e ___ g h ___

j k ___ m n ___ p q ___

s ___ u v ___ x y ___

Five-a-Day: Numbers to 10

Write how many.	Write how many.	Write how many.
🧸 🧸 🧸	🧸 🧸 🧸 🧸	🧸 🧸 🧸
_____	_____	_____

Write how many.	Write how many.
🧸 🧸 🧸 🧸	🧸 🧸 🧸
_____	_____

Sentence-a-Day

ben   has   a   red   bear

_____

- -

_____

Color Words

Color each picture the same color as in the phrase below it.

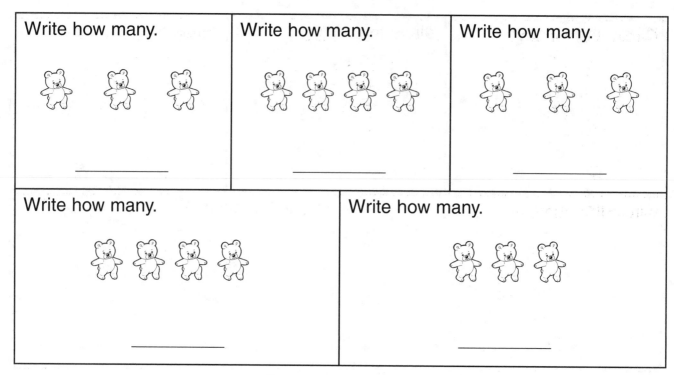

| a red apple | an orange basketball | a yellow banana |

Five-a-Day: Numbers to 10

Circle the number.	Circle the number.	Circle the number.
5 6	5 6	5 6

Circle the number.	Circle the number.
5 6	5 6

Sentence-a-Day

does   julieta   have   a   blue   bear

_____

- -

Color Words

Color each picture the same color as in the phrase below it.

a green grasshopper

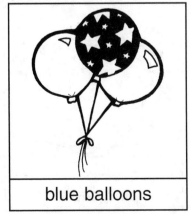

blue balloons

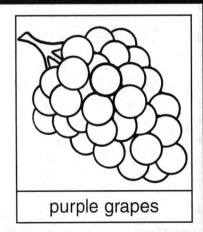

purple grapes

Five-a-Day: Numbers to 10

Write how many.	Write how many.	Write how many.

_____ _____ _____

Write how many.	Write how many.

_____ _____

Sentence-a-Day

samantha   has   a   purple   bear

Color Words

Color each picture the same color as in the phrase below it.

a brown bear

a pink cupcake

a black shirt

Five-a-Day: Numbers to 10

Circle the number.	Circle the number.	Circle the number.
0 1 2	3 4 5	4 5 6

Circle the number.	Circle the number.
1 2 3	4 5 6

Sentence-a-Day

lee   has   an   orange   bear

_____

- -

_____

Color Words

Color each picture the same color as in the phrase below it.

a white sheep

a gray elephant

a green turtle

Five-a-Day: Numbers to 10

Write how many.	Write how many.	Write how many.

_____

_____

_____

Write how many.	Write how many.

_____

_____

Sentence-a-Day

does   alex   have   a   gray   bear

_____

- -

Copy each number word onto the line.

zero _____

one _____

two _____

three _____

four _____

five _____

Five-a-Day: Numbers to 10

Circle the number.

6 7 8

Circle the number.

6 7 8

Circle the number.

7 8 9

Circle the number.

6 7 8

Circle the number.

6 7 8

Sentence-a-Day

does luis have a white cat

_____

- -

_____

 Copy each number word onto the line.

six _____

seven _____

eight _____

nine _____

ten _____

Five-a-Day: Numbers to 10

Write how many.	Write how many.	Write how many.
_____	_____	_____

Write how many.	Write how many.
_____	_____

Sentence-a-Day

juanita   has   a   black   cat

_____

- -

Day to Day

Draw a line to match the names of the days of the week.

Sunday	Wednesday
Monday	Saturday
Tuesday	Friday
Wednesday	Sunday
Thursday	Monday
Friday	Tuesday
Saturday	Thursday

Five-a-Day: Numbers to 10

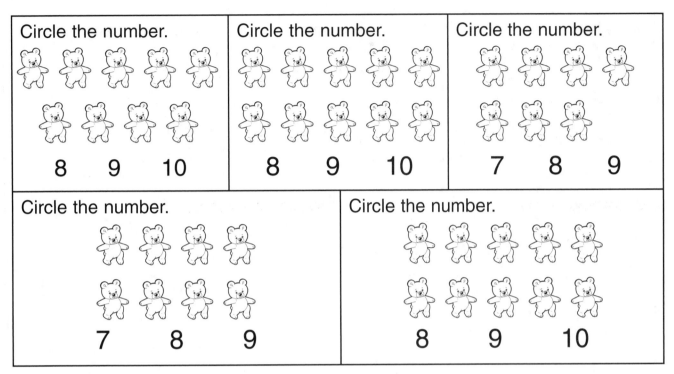

Circle the number.

8   9   10

Circle the number.

8   9   10

Circle the number.

7   8   9

Circle the number.

7   8   9

Circle the number.

8   9   10

Sentence-a-Day

my   mom   has   a   tan   cat

Write the name for each picture on the line below it.

| apple | bed | cat | dog | egg | fish |

Five-a-Day: Numbers to 10

Write how many.

_____

Write how many.

_____

Write how many.

_____

Write how many.

_____

Write how many.

_____

Sentence-a-Day

my   cat   is   yellow

_____

- -

_____

Write the name for each picture on the line below it.

| goose | hat | ice cream | jet | key | lion |

_____   _____   _____

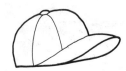

_____   _____   _____

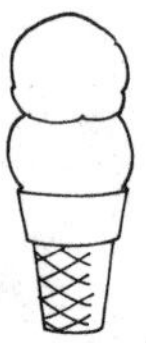

Five-a-Day: Numbers to 10

Write the number.	Write the number.	Write the number.
zero _____	two _____	four _____
one _____	three _____	five _____

Write the number.	Write the number.
six _____	eight _____
seven _____	nine _____

Sentence-a-Day

do   you   have   a   bear

_____

_____

Write the name for each picture on the line below it.

| mask | net | owl | pig | quilt | rabbit |

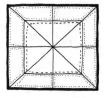 

_____   _____   _____

_____   _____   _____

Five-a-Day: Numbers to 10

Write the missing number.	Write the missing number.	Write the missing number.
0, 1, ___ , 3, 4	1, 2, ___ , 4, 5	5, 6, ___ , 8, 9

Write the missing number.	Write the missing number.
0, ___ ,2, 3, 4	___ ,1, 2, 3, 4

Sentence-a-Day

i   have   one   red   apple

Write the name for each picture on the line below it.

| snail   tree   unicorn   vest   wagon   x-ray |

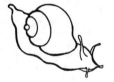

_____   _____   _____

_____   _____   _____

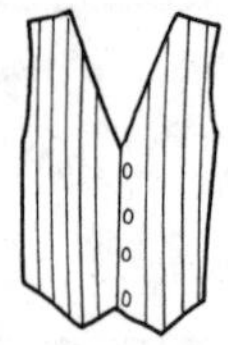

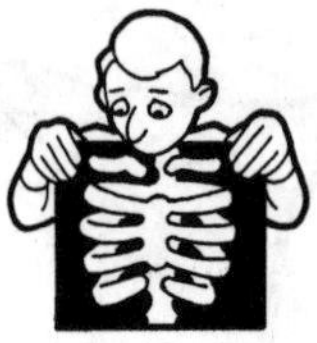

Five-a-Day: Add and Subtract to 6

Circle the group that has more.	Circle the group that has more.	Circle the group that has more.
★ ★ ★	★ ★ ★ ★	★ ★ ★ ★ ★ ★ ★ ★ ★ ★

Circle the group that has more.	Circle the group that has more.

★ ★ ★
  ★ ★   ★ ★
	★ ★ ★ ★ ★ ★ ★
	★ ★ ★ ★ ★ ★
	  ★ ★ ★ ★ ★

Sentence-a-Day

cassie   has   two   green   apples

_____

Write the name for each picture on the line below it.

| yarn | zebra | chair | shell | thumb | whale |

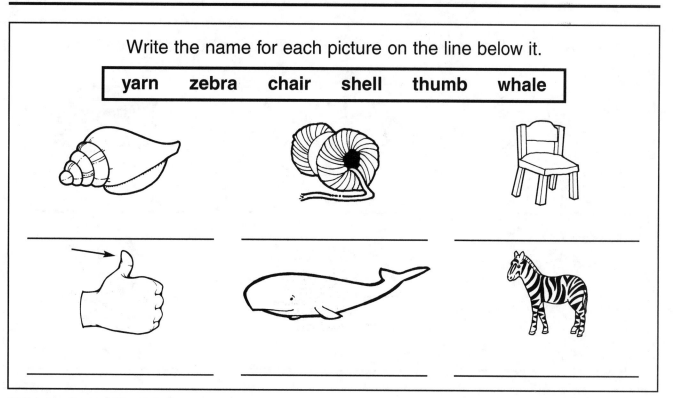

Five-a-Day: Add and Subtract to 6

Circle the group that has less.	Circle the group that has less.	Circle the group that has less.
★ ★ ★ ★ ★	★ ★ ★ ★ ★ ★ ★ ★ ★ ★	★ ★ ★ ★ ★ ★ ★

Circle the group that has less.	Circle the group that has less.
★ ★ ★ ★ ★ ★ ★ ★ ★ ★ ★	★ ★ ★ ★ ★ ★ ★ ★ ★ ★ ★

Sentence-a-Day

mr.   brown   has   three   trees

_____

- -

_____

Write the letters that make the beginning and ending sounds for each picture.

____ n ____   ____ a ____   ____ a ____

____ o ____   ____ g ____   ____ a ____

Five-a-Day: Numbers to 10

Write the missing number.	Write the missing number.	Write the missing number.
10, 9, ____ , 7, 6	5, 4, ____ , 2, 1	7, 6, 5, ____ , 3, 2

Write the missing number.	Write the missing number.
4, 3, 2, 1, ____	8, ____ , 6, 5, 4

Sentence-a-Day

grandma   Sue   has   four   yellow   apples

_____

- -

Write the letters that make the beginning and ending sounds for each picture.

___ ir ___

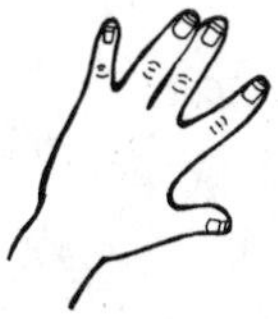

___ an ___

___ ce crea ___

____ e ___

___ in ___

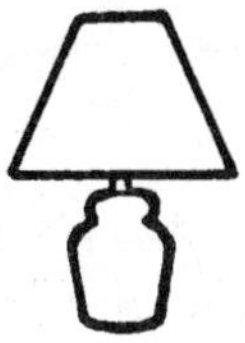

___ am ___

Five-a-Day: Patterns

Finish the pattern.	Finish the pattern.	Finish the pattern.
A, B, A, B, A, ___, ___, ___, ___, ___	C, D, C, D, C, ___, ___, ___, ___, ___	1, 2, 1, 2, 1, ___, ___, ___, ___, ___

Finish the pattern.	Finish the pattern.
3, 4, 5, 3, 4, 5, 3, 4, 5, 3, ___, ___, ___, ___, ___, ___, ___	E, F, G, E, F, G, E, F, G, E, ___, ___, ___, ___, ___, ___, ___

Sentence-a-Day

ms.   rosenberg   ate   five   apples

_____

- -

_____

Write the letters that make the beginning and ending sounds for each picture.

___ a ___

___ e ___

___ oa ___

___ ai ___

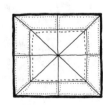
___ uil ___

___ abbi ___

Five-a-Day: Add and Subtract to 6

Draw a group that has 1 less.	Draw a group that has 1 more.	Draw a group that has 1 more.

Draw a group that has 1 more.	Draw a group that has 1 more.

Sentence-a-Day

do   you   have   six   trees

_____

- -

_____

Write the letters that make the beginning and ending sounds for each picture.

___ ig ___

___ en ___

___ nicor ___

___ es ___

___ e ___

___ ra ___

Five-a-Day: Tally Marks

Write the same number of tally marks.	Write the same number of tally marks.	Write the same number of tally marks.
|||	||||/ ||||	||||/ ||

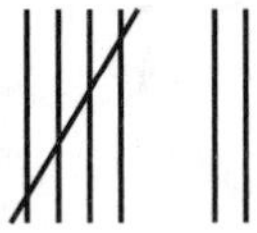

Write the same number of tally marks.	Write the same number of tally marks.
6	10

Sentence-a-Day

miguel   made   seven   apple   pies

_____

- -

_____

Write the letters that make the beginning and ending sounds for each picture.

____ ar ____

____ ebr ____

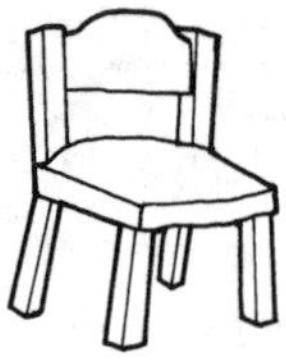

____ ai ____

____ ee ____

____ rea ____

____ ee ____

Five-a-Day: Add and Subtract to 6

Write how many in all.	Write how many in all.	Write how many in all.
🧸 + 🧸	🧸🧸 🧸🧸 + 🧸	🧸🧸🧸 🧸🧸 + 🧸🧸
_____	_____	_____

Write how many in all.	Write how many in all.
🧸🧸 + 🧸🧸	🧸 + 🧸🧸
_____	_____

Sentence-a-Day

juan   has   eight   small   apples

_____

- -

_____

SEPTEMBER

Sunday	Monday	Tuesday	Wednesday	Thursday	Friday	Saturday
				1	2	3
4	5	6	7	8	9	10
11	12	13	14	15	16	17
18	19	20	21	22	23	24
25	26	27	28	29	30	

1. What is the name of this month?

   _____

2. How many days are in September?

   _____

3. On what day of the week does September begin?

   _____

4. On what day of the week does September end?

   _____

Five-a-Day: Add and Subtract to 6

Write how many in all.	Write how many in all.	Write how many in all.
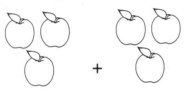	 +	
_____	_____	_____

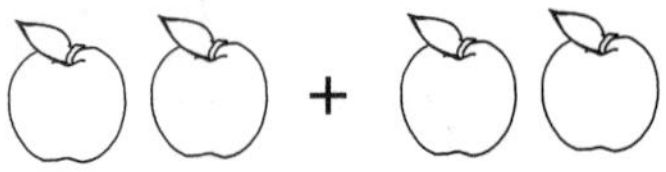

Write how many in all.	Write how many in all.
(apples) + (apples)	(apples) + (apple)
_____	_____

Sentence-a-Day

uncle   joe   has   nine   big   apples

_____

- -

_____

Count the number of apples. Write the number word on the line.

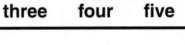

| zero | one | two | three | four | five |

_____   _____   _____

(apples)   (apples)   (apples)

_____   _____   _____

Five-a-Day: Add and Subtract to 6

$\begin{array}{r} 1 \\ +\ 0 \\ \hline \end{array}$	$\begin{array}{r} 2 \\ +\ 1 \\ \hline \end{array}$	$\begin{array}{r} 5 \\ +\ 1 \\ \hline \end{array}$

My sister bought 1 apple. Then she bought 2 more. How many apples did she buy in all? _____ apples in all.	My brother had 0 pies. Then he bought 6 pies. How many pies did he buy in all? _____ pies in all.

Sentence-a-Day

does   grandpa   eat   applesauce

_____

- -

_____

Count the number of apples. Write the number word on the line.

six   seven   eight   nine   ten

_____   _____   _____

_____   _____

Five-a-Day: Add and Subtract to 6

$$3 + 1$$ _____

$$4 + 2$$ _____

$$1 + 1$$ _____

Jenna had 3 apples already. She picked 3 more off of her apple tree. How many apples does Jenna have in all?

Jenna has _____ apples in all.

Carmine didn't have any apples. His friend Paulo gave him 1 apple. How many apples does Carmine have now?

Carmine has _____ apples now.

Sentence-a-Day

do   an   apple   have   seeds

_____

- -

_____

Read and follow the directions.

1. Color the apples on the ground green. How many apples did you color green?

   _____

2. Color the apples in the tree yellow. How many apples did you color yellow?

   _____

3. Color the apples on the fence red. How many apples did you color red? _____

4. Which apple color do you like best? _____

Five-a-Day: Add and Subtract to 6

Solve.	Solve.	Solve.
2 +3 ―――	4 +2 ―――	1 +2 ―――
_____ in all.	_____ in all.	_____ in all.

I had 4 small green apples. Jamie gave me 1 red apple. How many apples do I have in all?	Gary found 1 yellow apple on the ground. He found 1 green apple on the fence. How many apples did Gary find in all?
I have _____ apples in all.	Gary found _____ apples in all.

Sentence-a-Day

najene's   apple   has   a   brown   stem

_____

- -

_____

Word Bank

apples   ten   basket   eat   tasty

Use the words in the word bank to complete each sentence.

I see a _____ .

It is full of _____ .

I count more than _____ of them.

I like to _____ apples.

They are _____ .

Five-a-Day: Add and Subtract to 6

Solve. $\begin{array}{r} 3 \\ +2 \\ \hline \end{array}$	Solve. $\begin{array}{r} 2 \\ +2 \\ \hline \end{array}$	Solve. $\begin{array}{r} 1 \\ +5 \\ \hline \end{array}$
_____ in all.	_____ in all.	_____ in all.

Miranda bought 3 small apples and 1 large apple. How many apples did Miranda buy in all? Miranda bought _____ apples in all.	Sanda picked 1 apple. Clara picked 1 apple. How many apples did the girls pick in all? They picked _____ apples in all.

Sentence-a-Day

pierre's   apple   doesn't   have   a   stem

- -

_____

Write the name for each picture on the line below it.

| worm | blossom | tree | apple | basket | core |

_____   _____   _____

_____   _____   _____

Five-a-Day: Add and Subtract to 6

1 + 0 = _____	1 + 1 = _____	2 + 2 = _____
2 + 0 = _____	4 + 1 = _____	3 + 2 = _____

Marcy found 4 seeds in one pumpkin. She found 0 seeds in another pumpkin. How many seeds did Marcy find in all?

Marcy found _____ seeds in all.

Mark found 1 pumpkin seed in his pocket. He found 4 pumpkin seeds in his shoe. How many pumpkin seeds did Mark find in all?

Mark found _____ seeds in all.

Sentence-a-Day

louise   likes   small   pumpkins

_____

- -

_____

Following Directions

1. Color the rake yellow.

2. Color the tree trunk brown.

3. Color the bag of leaves black.

4. Color the pile of leaves orange.

5. Color the ground green.

6. Which color do you like best? _____

Five-a-Day: Add and Subtract to 6

Circle the answer.	Circle the answer.	Circle the answer.
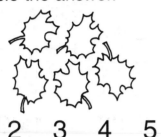		
2 3 4 5	2 3 4 5	2 3 4 5

Circle the answer.

Linda had 4 scarecrows. She bought 1 more. How many scarecrows does she have in all?

4   5   6   7

Circle the answer.

Johnny found 5 pumpkins in the hay loft. He found 2 more in the hay wagon. How many pumpkins did he find in all?

5   6   7   8

Sentence-a-Day

did   you   find   a   fat   pumpkin

_____

- -

OCTOBER						
Sunday	Monday	Tuesday	Wednesday	Thursday	Friday	Saturday
		1	2	3	4	5
6	7	8	9	10	11	12
13	14	15	16	17	18	19
20	21	22	23	24	25	26
27	28	29	30	31		

1. What is the name of this month? _____

2. How many days are in October?

   _____

3. On what day of the week is Halloween?

   _____

4. On what day does October end?

   _____

5. How many Sundays are in this month?

   _____

34

Name _____

Five-a-Day: Time

Circle the correct time.	Circle the correct time.	Circle the correct time.

3:00 9:00	6:00 12:00	8:00 4:00

| Phil goes to bed at 8:00 P.M. Make the clock show 8:00 P.M. |  | Marianne gets up at 6:00 A.M. Make the clock show 6:00 A.M. |  |

Sentence-a-Day

do   you   know   how   to   tell   time

- -

Write the name for each picture on the line below it.

cat   candy   hat   pumpkin   scarecrow   bat

_____ _____ _____

_____ _____ _____

Five-a-Day: Time

Write the time.  ___ ___ : ___ ___ ___	Write the time.  ___ ___ : ___ ___ ___	Write the time.  ___ ___ : ___ ___ ___

Raul takes a 1 hour nap each day. He fell asleep at 1:00. Make the clock show the time that Raul fell asleep.		Francesca went to the 3:00 movie. Make the clock show the time that the movie started. 

Sentence-a-Day

hank   know   how   to   tell   time

_____

- -

Word Bank

Use the words from the word bank to complete each sentence.

| jack-o-lantern   stem   green   round   orange   carved |

A pumpkin is _____ .

It has a brown _____ .

It has _____ leaves.

The pumpkin has an

_____ rind. When a

pumpkin is _____ , it

is called a _____ .

Five-a-Day: Time

Draw the hour hand.	Draw the hour hand.	Draw the hour hand.
 9:00	 7:00	 6:00

I played with my puppy for 1 hour. We began at 4:00. Make the clock show the time that we finished playing. 	It takes me 1 hour to get ready for school. I started getting ready at 7:00. Make the clock show the time I was ready for school. 

Sentence-a-Day

what   time   are   it

_____

- -

_____

Word Bank

| on top of   in front of   under   beside |

Use the words from the word bank to complete each sentence.

The cat is _____ the tree.

The tree is _____ the fence.

The jack-o-lantern is _____ the fence.

The leaf is _____ the fence.

© Teacher Created Materials, Inc.   37   #2514 Daily Skills Practice

Five-a-Day: Time

Draw both hands.	Draw both hands.	Draw both hands.
		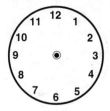
6:00	8:00	10:00

Make the clock show 1 hour later. Write the time.		Make the clock show 3 hours later. Write the time.	
	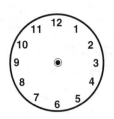		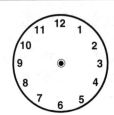
11:00 ___ ___ : ___ ___		4:00 ___ ___ : ___ ___	

Sentence-a-Day

do   alice   know   how   to   tell   time

_____

- -

_____

Find the words hidden in the word search. Color each hidden word when you find it.

X	L	E	A	V	E	S	H	F	T
K	B	L	A	C	K	F	Q	P	L
M	C	A	T	P	Q	W	V	Q	S
S	C	A	R	E	C	R	O	W	O
J	E	T	C	A	N	D	Y	O	X
O	C	T	O	B	E	R	G	E	P
S	P	H	A	Y	J	M	C	T	P
Q	R	U	D	F	A	L	L	O	W
X	P	S	O	R	A	N	G	E	B
P	U	M	P	K	I	N	R	Z	I

1. black
2. candy
3. cat
4. fall
5. hay
6. leaves
7. October
8. orange
9. pumpkin
10. scarecrow

Five-a-Day: Time

Draw the hands to show one hour later.

12:00   __ : __ __

Draw the hands to show one hour later.

9:00   __ __ : __ __

Draw the hands to show one hour later.

4:00   __ : __ __

Draw the hands to show one hour later.

1:00   __ : __ __

Draw the hands to show one hour later.

8:00   __ : __ __

Sentence-a-Day

i   thinks   she   does

_____

- -

_____

Name the parts of the scarecrow. Write the correct word on each line.

1. pumpkin
2. face
3. hat
4. leg
5. arm

Five-a-Day: Add and Subtract to 6

Subtract.	Subtract.	Subtract.
$\begin{array}{r} 4 \\ -\ 2 \\ \hline \end{array}$	$\begin{array}{r} 3 \\ -\ 1 \\ \hline \end{array}$	$\begin{array}{r} 5 \\ -\ 2 \\ \hline \end{array}$

Solve.	Solve.
$\begin{array}{r} 5 \\ -\ 2 \\ \hline \end{array}$ ● ● ● ⊗ ⊗ _____ are left.	$\begin{array}{r} 4 \\ -\ 2 \\ \hline \end{array}$ ● ● ⊗ ⊗ _____ are left.

Sentence-a-Day

we   is   learning   to   tell   time

_____

- -

Word Bank

minutes   seconds   time   hours

Use the words in the word bank to complete each sentence.

A clock helps people keep track of

_____ .

There are 24 _____ in one day.

There are 60 _____ in one hour.

There are 60 _____ in one minute.

What time does the clock show? _____

Five-a-Day: Add and Subtract to 6

Add.	Subtract.	Add.
4 + 0 _____	5 + 0 _____	2 + 1 _____

Solve.

There are 5 frogs. If 2 frogs hop away, how many are left?

There are _____ frogs left.

Solve.

There are 6 geese. If 1 goose flies away, how many are left?

There are _____ geese left.

Sentence-a-Day

ms.   redford   she   can   tell   time

_____

- -

_____

Read the scrambled sentence. Write the words in the correct order.

bottle.   The   a   bear   has

_____

- -

_____

Five-a-Day: Add and Subtract to 6

Solve.	Solve.	Solve.
$2 + 3 =$ _____	$1 + 4 =$ _____	$0 + 5 =$ _____
$3 - 2 =$ _____	$4 - 1 =$ _____	$5 - 0 =$ _____

Solve.

$$\begin{array}{r} 4 \\ -\ 3 \\ \hline \end{array}$$ run away.

_____ is left.

Solve.

$$\begin{array}{r} 5 \\ -\ 2 \\ \hline \end{array}$$ run away.

_____ are left.

Sentence-a-Day

a   watch   keep   track   of   the   time

_____

- -

Find each of the hidden words. Color in each word.

M	O	R	N	I	N	G	E	C	W
E	V	E	N	I	N	G	W	T	E
I	C	B	Q	V	O	L	K	H	M
N	D	I	T	I	V	Y	W	S	H
Y	D	B	C	L	O	C	K	U	N
H	O	U	R	P	Y	B	W	R	I
C	N	T	I	M	E	F	H	X	O
H	A	N	D	S	W	A	T	C	H
R	S	E	C	O	N	D	C	M	J
M	I	N	U	T	E	M	U	N	J

1. clock
2. evening
3. hands
4. hour
5. minute
6. morning
7. second
8. time
9. watch

Name _____

Five-a-Day: Add and Subtract to 6

Circle the correct math sentence.	Circle the correct math sentence.	Circle the correct math sentence.

3 + 2 = 5 3 − 2 = 1	4 + 1 = 5 5 − 1 = 4	2 + 1 = 3 2 − 1 = 1

Write the addition sentence.	Write the subtraction sentence.

_____ + _____ = _____	_____ − _____ = _____

Sentence-a-Day

me   watch   beeps   every   hour

_____

- -

The words in the sentence below have been scrambled. Write the words in the correct order.

ringing!   alarm   The   is   clock

_____

- -

_____

Five-a-Day: Add and Subtract to 6

Write the missing number.	Write the missing number.	Write the missing number.
$2 + \underline{\hspace{1cm}} = 3$	$5 - \underline{\hspace{1cm}} = 1$	$6 - \underline{\hspace{1cm}} = 3$

Jake went fishing. He caught 6 fish in the morning and 0 fish in the afternoon. How many fish did Jake catch in all? $\underline{\hspace{1cm}} + \underline{\hspace{1cm}} = \underline{\hspace{1cm}}$	Ali caught 4 salmon. She gave 3 to the Trout family. How many salmon does Ali have left? $\underline{\hspace{1cm}} - \underline{\hspace{1cm}} = \underline{\hspace{1cm}}$

Sentence-a-Day

aunt   claudia   collect   fishing   poles

_____

- -

Use the words in the word bank to label the parts of the clock.

Word Bank

hour hand   number   alarm   minute hand

44   © Teacher Created Materials, Inc.

Five-a-Day: Add and Subtract to 10

Add.

5 + 2 = _____

Add.

7 + 0 = _____

Add.

6 + 1 = _____

Dave ate 3 doughnuts for breakfast. He ate 4 more doughnuts for snack. How many doughnuts did Dave eat in all?	Saed has 5 books. He checked out 3 more books from the library. How many books does Saed have in all?
_____ + _____ = _____	_____ + _____ = _____

Sentence-a-Day

uncle   herman   are   always   late

_____

- -

_____

Read the scrambled sentence. Write the words in the correct order.

bats   The   flying.   are

_____

- -

_____

Five-a-Day: Add and Subtract to 10

Add.	Add.	Add.
6 + 1 ___	5 + 2 ___	7 + 0 ___

My grandpa fixed 3 clocks yesterday and 7 clocks today. How many clocks did my grandpa fix in all?	On Greg's birthday, he received 5 watches. Greg already had 1 watch. How many watches does Greg have in all?
_____ + _____ = _____	_____ + _____ = _____

Sentence-a-Day

he   don't   know   how   to   tell   time

Read the scrambled sentence. Write the words in the correct order.

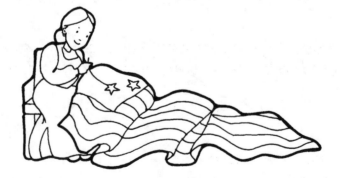

making   The   is   woman   flag.   a

_____

- -

_____

Name _____

Name _____

Five-a-Day: Add and Subtract to 10

Add.	Add.	Add.

$5 + 3 = $ _____

$7 + 1 = $ _____

$2 + 6 = $ _____

Billy and I were outside one night. Billy saw 4 bats and I saw 5 bats. How many bats did we see in all?	Susanne has 3 bat houses. Tasia has 6 bat houses. How many bat houses do Susanne and Tasia have in all?
_____ + _____ = _____	_____ + _____ = _____

Sentence-a-Day

is   all   bats   black

_____

- -

_____

Read the story about bats and answer the questions that follow.

Bats are nocturnal mammals. Nocturnal means they are active at night and rest during the day.

Bats are also mammals. Bats are mammals because they are warm-blooded, born alive, have lungs, and have hair on their bodies.

 1. When are bats active? _____

 2. Is a bat a member of the bird family?

_____

 3. Name one characteristic that all bats have that make them a member of the mammal family.

_____

Five-a-Day: Add and Subtract to 10

Add.	Add.	Add.
2 + 6 ___	1 + 3 ___	3 + 4 ___

Aunt Clara once saw 3 fruit bats and 2 fish-eating bats. How many bats did Aunt Clara see in all? _____ + _____ = _____	On Monday, Uncle Sean saw 5 brown bats. On Tuesday he saw some more brown bats. He saw 10 bats in all. How many bats did he see on Tuesday? _____ + _____ = _____

Sentence-a-Day

let's   ask   mr.   montoya

_____

- -

_____

Find each of the hidden words. Color in each word.

B	A	T	F	I	N	G	E	R	S
P	I	N	S	E	C	T	S	R	V
S	M	F	T	M	L	Y	T	C	P
N	O	C	T	U	R	N	A	L	K
T	P	O	J	D	F	L	U	N	Z
T	I	E	M	A	M	M	A	L	R
M	B	S	N	D	Y	D	X	S	H
L	H	E	A	R	I	N	G	B	Z
R	D	W	V	P	S	K	I	N	E
E	W	I	N	G	S	V	M	E	N

1. bat
2. fingers
3. hearing
4. insects
5. mammal
6. nocturnal
7. skin
8. wings

Five-a-Day: Add and Subtract to 10

Add.	Add.	Add.

3 + 1 = _____

6 + 1 = _____

4 + 1 = _____

Eddie has 2 purple bat rings and 7 green bat rings. How many bat rings does Eddie have in all?

_____ + _____ = _____

Ariel once caught 3 bats in a net and 4 bats in a box. How many bats did Ariel catch in all?

_____ + _____ = _____

Sentence-a-Day

he   know   everything   about   bats

_____

- -

Read the story about bats and circle the answers to the questions.

Bats are not dangerous to people. In fact, bats help people out by eating insects like mosquitoes. One bat can eat hundreds of mosquitoes in one night.

But, if you ever see a bat on the ground, "don't pick it up!" If a bat is lying on the ground, it means that bat is sick or injured. Call the local zoo or the animal shelter and let them take care of the bat.

1. Are bats dangerous to people? Yes No

2. What do bats like to eat? hamburgers mosquitoes

3. What should you do if you see a bat on the ground?
   pick it up
   call the zoo or animal shelter

4. Do you like bats?
   Yes No

Five-a-Day: Add and Subtract to 10

Add.	Add.	Add.

4 + 5 = _____	6 + 2 = _____	7 + 2 = _____

Amy made 1 scarecrow. Her friend gave her 8 more. How many scarecrows does Amy have in all?	Alistair planted 9 rows of corn on Thursday. He didn't plant any corn on Friday. How many rows of corn did Alistair plant in all?
_____ + _____ = _____	_____ + _____ = _____

Sentence-a-Day

has   you   ever   seen   a   bat

_____

- -

_____

Word Bank

Use the words in the word bank to label the parts of a bat.

| wing | body | ear | tail | eye | leg |

Name _____

Five-a-Day: Add and Subtract to 10

Solve.

$5 + 4$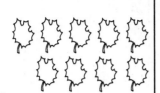

_____ leaves in all.

Solve.

$4 + 4$

_____ trees in all.

Solve.

$6 + 2$

_____ stars in all.

Sally put up 5 tents. Rob put up 2 tents. How many tents did they put up in all?

_____ + _____ = _____

Zach saw 3 stars in the night sky. Rosie saw 6 stars. How many stars did they see in all?

_____ + _____ = _____

Sentence-a-Day

does   you   family   like   to   camp

_____

- -

_____

Unscramble each word. Write the word correctly on the line.

rbea

low

tfores

elak

_____

hfis

pcam

etre

tnet

_____   _____   _____   _____

Five-a-Day: Add and Subtract to 10

Add.	Add.	Add.
7 + 2 ———	3 + 5 ———	2 + 7 ———

Barney has 2 apples. He bought 5 more. How many apples does Barney have in all?

_____ + _____ = _____

Christie has 3 lemons and 4 limes. How many lemons and limes does Christie have in all?

_____ + _____ = _____

Sentence-a-Day

me   likes   the   yellow   corn   best

Which foods grow on the ground and which foods grow on trees? Write each food name in the correct category.

Foods That Grow on the Ground

1. _____

2. _____

3. _____

Foods That Grow on Trees

1. _____

2. _____

3. _____

coconut

mushroom

onion

lemon

carrot

apple

Name _____

Five-a-Day: Add and Subtract to 10

Add.

____ + ____ = ____

Add.

____ + ____ = ____

Add.

____ + ____ = ____

Diego lit 2 lanterns in the first tent. Diego then lit 6 lanterns in the second tent. How many lanterns did Diego light in all?

____ + ____ = ____ lanterns lit in all.

Emily found 1 stick while on her morning walk. She later found 8 sticks while on her evening walk. How many sticks did Emily find in all?

____ + ____ = ____ sticks in all.

Sentence-a-Day

can   you   makes   popcorn   out   of   corn

_____

Use the words in the word bank to label the parts of a tree.

Word Bank

branch   leaves   roots   trunk

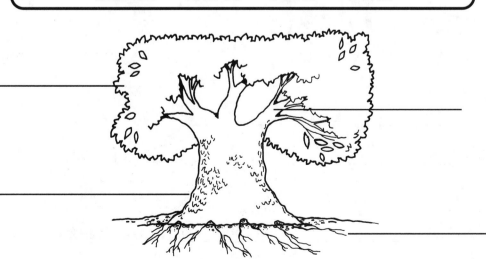

Five-a-Day: Add and Subtract to 10

Subtract.	Subtract.	Subtract.
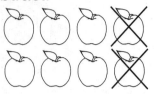		
____ – ____ = ____	____ – ____ = ____	____ – ____ = ____

Georgia has 7 pieces of corn. She ate 4 pieces of corn. How many pieces did she have left? ____ – ____ = ____ pieces of corn.	Enrique made 9 corn tortillas. He gave 1 corn tortilla to Herman. How many tortillas does Enrique have left? ____ – ____ = ____ tortillas left.

Sentence-a-Day

i   knows   you   can   make   corn   tortillas

_____

What does each farm animal give us? Complete each sentence with the correct word.

chicken   cow   pig   sheep

A _____ gives us milk.

A _____ gives us wool.

A _____ gives us ham.

A _____ gives us eggs.

Name _____

Five-a-Day: Add and Subtract to 10

Subtract.	Subtract.	Subtract.

8 – 2 = _____	7 – 4 = _____	8 – 3 = _____

Ms. Grain has 8 turkeys on her farm. She sold 6 of the turkeys. How many turkeys does Ms. Grain have left?	Larry stacked up 8 bales of hay. If 4 of the bales fell over, how many bales of hay are left in the stack?
_____ – _____ = _____ turkeys left.	_____ – _____ = _____ are in the stack.

Sentence-a-Day

do   tony   like   turkey

_____

- -

_____

Circle the correct word that goes with each picture.

dog dogs   horse horses   cat cats

dog dogs   horse horses   cat cats

Name _____

Five-a-Day: Add and Subtract to 10

Subtract. $\begin{array}{r}9\\-3\\\hline\end{array}$	Subtract. $\begin{array}{r}7\\-2\\\hline\end{array}$	Subtract. $\begin{array}{r}6\\-4\\\hline\end{array}$

There were 9 children playing outside. If 8 children went inside, how many children stayed outside playing? _____ – _____ = _____ child.	Mom placed 8 pumpkin pies were sitting on the window sill. The dog ate 4 of them. How many pies are left? _____ – _____ = _____ pies were left.

Sentence-a-Day

jay   think   a   spider   has   eight   legs

_____

NOVEMBER

Sunday	Monday	Tuesday	Wednesday	Thursday	Friday	Saturday
	1	2	3	4	5	6
7	8	9	10	11	12	13
14	15	16	17	18	19	20
21	22	23	24	25	26	27
28	29	30				

1. What is the name of this month? _____

2. How many days are in this month? _____

3. On what day of the week is Thanksgiving? _____

4. On what day of the week is November 11? _____

5. How many Sundays are there in November? _____

Five-a-Day: Add and Subtract to 10

Subtract.	Subtract.	Subtract.
6 − 3 ———	7 − 5 ———	3 − 2 ———

Uncle Roberto made 1 cornucopia. He sold it. How many cornucopias does Uncle Roberto have left? ____ − ____ = ____ cornucopia.	Soua made 4 pumpkin pies for her family. Soua's family ate 2 pumpkin pies. How many pumpkin pies does Soua have left? ____ − ____ = ____ pies left.

Sentence-a-Day

mr.   vang   made   a   turkey   dinner

_____

- -

_____

Write the name for each picture on the line below it.

| corn | Pilgrim | Indian | turkey | Mayflower | pie |

_____   _____   _____

_____   _____   _____

Five-a-Day: Add and Subtract to 10

Subtract.	Subtract.	Subtract.
8 − 1 ___	2 − 2 ___	4 − 2 ___

Nekesha collects feathers. Yesterday she collected 7 yellow feathers. She dropped 4 of them on her way home. How many feathers does Nekesha have left? _____ − _____ = _____ feathers left.	Omar saw 7 turkeys sitting on the gate. If 3 of the turkeys flew away, how many turkeys were left? _____ − _____ = _____ turkeys left.

Sentence-a-Day

ms.   yang's   turkey   it   makes   lot   of   noise

_____

- -

Thanksgiving Dinner

Use the words from the word bank to label each part of the picture.

Word Bank

| table   chair   candle   dinner   place mat |

58

Five-a-Day: Add and Subtract to 10

Subtract.	Subtract.	Subtract.
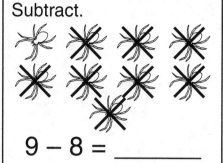	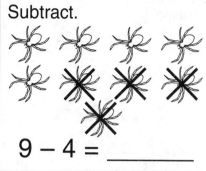	
9 – 5 = _____	9 – 8 = _____	9 – 4 = _____

Vivian gave her pet turkey 9 pieces of straw. The turkey ate 2 pieces of straw. How many pieces of straw are left? _____ – _____ = _____ pieces left.	Noel saw 9 spiders in the hay loft. If 3 of them were spinning webs, how many spiders were not spinning webs? _____ – _____ = _____ spiders.

Sentence-a-Day

how   many   legs   do   a   spider   have

_____

- -

Find each of the hidden words. Color in each word.

P	M	A	Y	F	L	O	W	E	R
E	N	G	L	A	N	D	S	B	R
Z	I	O	H	E	C	W	W	T	E
I	C	B	Q	V	O	L	K	H	M
N	D	I	T	U	R	K	E	Y	T
I	N	D	I	A	N	I	V	Y	W
S	H	T	H	A	N	K	F	U	L
P	I	L	G	R	I	M	Y	D	B
U	F	E	A	S	T	N	P	Y	B
F	R	I	E	N	D	S	W	R	I

1. England

2. feast

3. friends

4. Indian

5. Mayflower

6. Pilgrim

7. thankful

8. turkey

Five-a-Day: Add and Subtract to 10

Subtract.	Subtract.	Subtract.
★ ★ ★ ★ ★ ★ ✳ ✳ ✳ ✳ ____ – ____ = ____	★ ★ ★ ✳ ★ ★ ★ ✳ ____ – ____ = ____	✳ ✳ ✳ ✳ ✳ ✳ ✳ ✳ ★ ____ – ____ = ____

When I was cleaning my room, I found 8 red socks. I took 4 of them to the laundry room. How many red socks do I still have in my room? ____ – ____ = ____ red socks left.	Jerry unpacked the house lights. There were 9 lights. If 6 of the lights were broken, how many lights were not broken? ____ – ____ = ____ unbroken lights.

Sentence-a-Day

joanie   and   adam   likes   blue   lights

_____

- -

Nouns name people, places, and things. Circle the noun that names a person in each of the following sentences.

1. **Reginald is reading.**

2. **Lionel is playing.**

3. **Teddy is climbing.**

4. **Lizzy is sleeping.**

5. **Will is singing.**

Five-a-Day: Add and Subtract to 10

Add.	Subtract.	Add.
3 + 2 = _____	5 − 3 = _____	6 + 2 = _____
2 + 3 = _____	5 − 2 = _____	2 + 6 = _____

Timmy had 8 green marbles. He gave 6 marbles to his friend Mateo. How many marbles does Timmy have left? _____ − _____ = _____ marbles left.	Jessie bought 2 stickers. Her father gave her some stickers. Now Jessie has 6 stickers in all. How many stickers did her father give her? 2 + _____ = 6 stickers in all.

Sentence-a-Day

they   singed   a   song   about   lights

_____

- -

_____

Nouns name people, places, and things. Circle the noun that names a thing in each of the following sentences.

1. **The mop is old and dirty.**

2. **Where is the orange house?**

3. **Who ate all of the pizza?**

4. **The t-shirt is ripped.**

5. **The dog is hungry.**

Five-a-Day: Add and Subtract to 10

Solve.

$$\begin{array}{r} 7 \\ + 2 \\ \hline \end{array}$$

_____ in all.

Solve.

$$\begin{array}{r} 8 \\ + 2 \\ \hline \end{array}$$

_____ in all.

Solve.

$$\begin{array}{r} 2 \\ + 7 \\ \hline \end{array}$$

_____ in all.

Uncle Jethro collects hats. He has 9 hats. He gave 7 to his nephew. How many hats does Uncle Jethro have left?

_____ – _____ = _____ hats left.

Daisy made 8 pink bows and 1 yellow bow. How many bows in all did Daisy make?

_____ + _____ = _____ bows in all.

Sentence-a-Day

does   you   think   the   lights   are   pretty

_____

- -

_____

Nouns name people, places, and things. Circle the noun that names a place in each of the following sentences.

1. **The park is full of people.**

2. **We went to San Francisco for the weekend.**

3. **Mr. Jenkins needs to go to the grocery store.**

4. **We live in Fresno.**

5. **The space ship is going to the moon.**

Five-a-Day: Add and Subtract to 10

Solve.	Solve.	Solve.
$3 + \underline{\hspace{1cm}} = 5$	$2 + \underline{\hspace{1cm}} = 6$	$0 + \underline{\hspace{1cm}} = 7$
$2 + \underline{\hspace{1cm}} = 5$	$4 + \underline{\hspace{1cm}} = 6$	$7 + \underline{\hspace{1cm}} = 7$

My grandma made 4 fruit cakes. My mother made 5 fruit cakes. How many fruit cakes did they make in all?	My dad baked 5 hams. My grandpa baked 4 hams. How many hams did they bake in all?
_____ + _____ = _____ fruit cakes.	_____ + _____ = _____ hams in all.

Sentence-a-Day

mark   and   martin   was   chasing   a   turkey

_____

- -

_____

Use one of these nouns to complete each sentence.

> **Shelly   home   Main Street   Herman   popcorn**

1. _____ went to the movies.

2. The movie theater was on _____ .

3. She ate lots of _____ .

4. After the movie, she went _____ .

5. She played with her brother, _____ .

Five-a-Day: Add and Subtract to 10

Circle the correct answer.	Circle the correct answer.	Circle the correct answer.
$8 - 4 =$ ___	$3 + 0 =$	$8 -$ ___ $= 3$
3 4 5 6	0 1 2 3	4 5 6 7

Suzy gathered 2 orange leaves. Then she gathered some brown leaves. She now has 7 leaves in all. How many brown leaves did she gather?	Brad picked several small poinsettias. He picked 2 large poinsettias. He now has 5 poinsettias. How many small poinsettias did Brad pick?
$2 +$ ____ $= 7$	____ $+ 2 = 5$

Sentence-a-Day

is   roses   red   or   green

_____

- -

_____

Use one of these nouns to complete each sentence.

paper   Walker   shoes   dinner   shoe store

1. Mr. _____ went to work.

2. He works at a _____ .

3. He sells _____ .

4. When he returns home, he likes to read the _____ .

5. Mr. Walker then eats _____ .

Five-a-Day: Place Value

Draw more than 10 circles.	Draw less than 10 circles.	Draw exactly 10 circles.

Circle the group with less than 10 stars.

★ ★ ★ ★ ★   ★ ★
★ ★ ★ ★   ★
★ ★   ★ ★

Circle the group with more than 9 stars

★ ★ ★   ★ ★ ★ ★ ★
★ ★ ★   ★ ★ ★ ★ ★
★ ★   ★ ★ ★ ★

Sentence-a-Day

six   people   is   in   taylor's   family

Find each of the hidden words. Color in each word.

S	U	N	D	A	Y	A	X	H	H
P	R	T	H	U	R	S	D	A	Y
V	S	A	T	U	R	D	A	Y	S
M	F	T	M	L	Y	T	C	P	K
T	P	O	J	D	F	L	U	N	Z
W	E	D	N	E	S	D	A	Y	T
I	E	R	M	B	S	N	D	Y	D
X	F	R	I	D	A	Y	S	H	L
T	U	E	S	D	A	Y	B	Z	R
D	M	O	N	D	A	Y	W	V	P

1. Sunday
2. Monday
3. Tuesday
4. Wednesday
5. Thursday
6. Friday
7. Saturday

Five-a-Day: Place Value

Circle 10 bears.  How many are left?____	Circle 10 cats.  How many are left?____	Circle 10 dogs. How many are left?____

Circle groups of 10 socks. How many groups of 10 can you make? How many single ones are left?  tens: _____ ones: _____	Circle groups of 10 pies. How many groups of 10 can you make? How many single ones are left? tens: _____ ones: _____

Sentence-a-Day

how   many   people   is   in   you   family

_____

An abbreviation is a short way to write a long word. Look at the days of the week. Draw a line to match each day's name to its abbreviation.

Sunday	**Fri.**
Monday	**Mon.**
Tuesday	**Sun.**
Wednesday	**Thurs.**
Thursday	**Sat.**
Friday	**Tues.**
Saturday	**Wed.**

Name _____

Five-a-Day: Place Value

What number comes before?	What number comes before?	What number comes before?
_____ , 10	_____ , 14	_____ , 8
_____ , 16	_____ , 11	_____ , 2

How many groups of ten are there?	How many groups of ten are there?

_____ tens = _____ ones	_____ tens = _____ ones

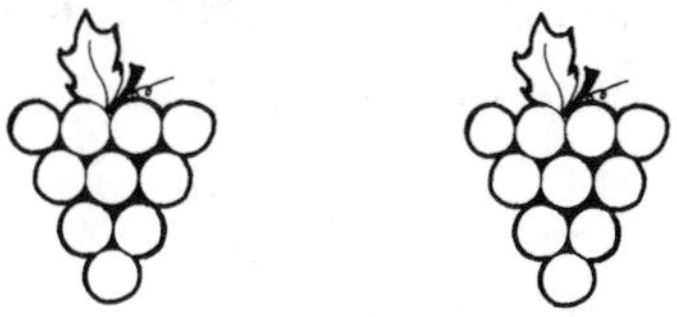

Sentence-a-Day

how   many   laps   did   charlie   run

_____

- -

_____

Write the abbreviation for each day of the week.

Sunday _____

Monday _____

Tuesday _____

Wednesday _____

Thursday _____

Friday _____

Saturday _____

Five-a-Day: Place Value

Write the number that comes in between.	Write the number that comes in between.	Write the number that comes in between.
11, _____ , 13	9, _____ , 11	3, _____ , 5
18, _____ , 20	0, _____ , 2	14, _____ , 16

I am the number that comes in between 12 and 14. What number am I?	I am the number that comes in between 16 and 18. What number am I?
_____	_____

Sentence-a-Day

jason   he   think   charlie   ran   eight   laps

_____

- -

The days of the week are scrambled. Use the numbers 1–7 to put them back in the correct order.

_____ **Saturday**

_____ **Thursday**

_____ **Monday**

_____ **Wednesday**

_____ **Sunday**

_____ **Friday**

_____ **Tuesday**

Five-a-Day: Place Value

What number comes after?	What number comes after?	What number comes after?
17, _____	8, _____	19, _____
2, _____	0, _____	1, _____

I am the number that comes after 9. What number am I?	I am the number that comes after 5. What number am I?
_____	_____

Sentence-a-Day

can   shelly   runs   more   than   that

_____

- -

_____

Put the names of the days of the week in alphabetical order.

Sunday	Monday	Tuesday	Wednesday
Thursday	Friday	Saturday	

A
B
C

1. _____
2. _____
3. _____
4. _____
5. _____
6. _____
7. _____

A
B
C

Five-a-Day: Place Value

Count the groups of 10 and write the number.	Count the groups of 10 and write the number.	Count the groups of 10 and write the number.

_____ tens =_____ ones	_____ tens =_____ ones	_____ tens =_____ ones

How many groups of 10 are there? How many ones are left?	How many groups of 10 are there? How many ones are left?

_____ tens _____ ones	_____ tens _____ ones

Sentence-a-Day

does   snowmen   have   feet

_____

- -

_____

Nouns are words that name people, places, or things. Draw a line to match each person to the correct noun.

boy   fire fighter   girl   police officer   teacher   mail carrier

Five-a-Day: Place Value

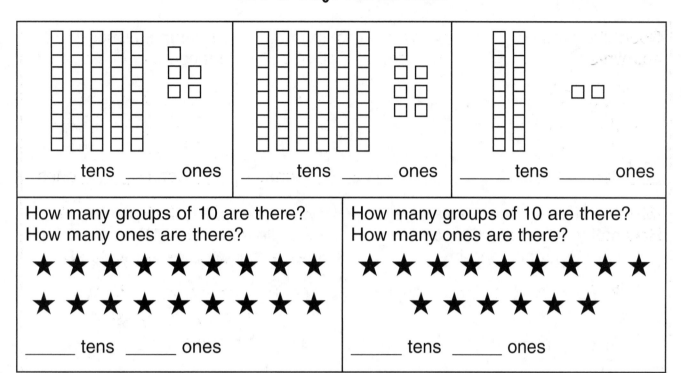

_____ tens _____ ones

_____ tens _____ ones

_____ tens _____ ones

How many groups of 10 are there?
How many ones are there?

★ ★ ★ ★ ★ ★ ★ ★ ★ ★
★ ★ ★ ★ ★ ★ ★ ★ ★ ★

_____ tens _____ ones

How many groups of 10 are there?
How many ones are there?

★ ★ ★ ★ ★ ★ ★ ★ ★ ★
★ ★ ★ ★ ★ ★

_____ tens _____ ones

Sentence-a-Day

is   there   any   tall   penguins

_____

- -

Nouns are words that name people, places, or things. Draw a line to match each place to the correct noun.

airport   lake   farm   zoo   tree house   school

Name _____

Five-a-Day: Place Value

Write the missing numbers.	Write the missing numbers.	Write the missing numbers.
17, 18, 19, _____, 21, 22, _____, 24	22, ___, 24, ___, 26, ___, ___, 29	10, 11, 12, ___, ___, ___, ___

Mystery Number: I am greater than 10 and less than 14. I am an even number. What number am I? The mystery number is _____ .	Mystery Number: I am greater than 15 and less than 25. When you count by tens you say my name. What number am I? The mystery number is _____ .

Sentence-a-Day

has   julian   made   a   snowman

_____

- -

_____

Nouns are words that name people, places, or things. Draw a line to match each picture to the correct noun.

fish   shell   dog   spider   chair   tree

Five-a-Day: Place Value

Circle each group of 10.	Circle each group of 10.	Circle each group of 10.
★ ★ ★ ★ ★ ★ ★ ★ ★ ★ ★ ★ ★ ★ ★ ★ _____ tens _____ ones	★ ★ ★ ★ ★ ★ ★ ★ ★ ★ ★ ★ ★ ★ ★ _____ tens _____ ones	★ ★ ★ ★ ★ ★ ★ ★ ★ ★ ★ ★ _____ tens _____ ones

Write down the number of tens and ones.	Write down the number of tens and ones.
37 _____ tens _____ ones	52 _____ tens _____ ones

Sentence-a-Day

mom   say   he   did   on   sunday

_____

- -

Nouns name people, places, or things. Look at the pictures. Write each picture's name in the correct category.

fish   **forest**   **park**   **phone**   **friends**   **clown**

People	**Places**	**Things**
1. _____	1. _____	1. _____
2. _____	2. _____	2. _____

Five-a-Day: Add and Subtract to 6

Sal made 6 pizzas. He sold 3. How many are left?	Paul made 4 hats. He made 2 more. How many hats did Paul make?	Jan put 7 cookies in a box. She took 2 out. How many cookies are in the box?
_____ − _____ = _____	_____ + _____ = _____	_____ − _____ = _____

Dale made 2 red hearts. Then he made 2 more. How many hearts did Dale make in all?	Dave made 5 apple pies. He sold 1 pie. How many pies does Dave have left?
_____ + _____ = _____ hearts in all.	_____ − _____ = _____ pies left.

Sentence-a-Day

is   there   ten   days   in   a   month

_____

Read the scrambled sentence. Write the words in the correct order.

children   on   board.   The   are   the   writing

_____

_____

Five-a-Day: Comparing Numbers

Circle the greater number.	Circle the greater number.	Circle the greater number.
10 6	29 38	16 12

Circle the greater number.	Circle the greater number.
70 72	10 19

Sentence-a-Day

our   town   it   has   many   farms

_____

- -

_____

Write the name for each picture on the line below it.
Word Bank

carrots   celery   cherries   corn   eggs   grapes

_____   _____   _____

_____   _____   _____

Name ____________________ **Practice 72**

Five-a-Day: Comparing Numbers

Circle the smaller number.	Circle the smaller number.	Circle the smaller number.
82 94	41 30	59 78

Write a number that is smaller than 24.	Write a number that is smaller than 65.
____________	____________

Sentence-a-Day

don't your uncle elroy have a farm

____

Put the farm animals in alphabetical order.

1. ____________
2. ____________
3. ____________
4. ____________
5. ____________
6. ____________
7. ____________
8. ____________

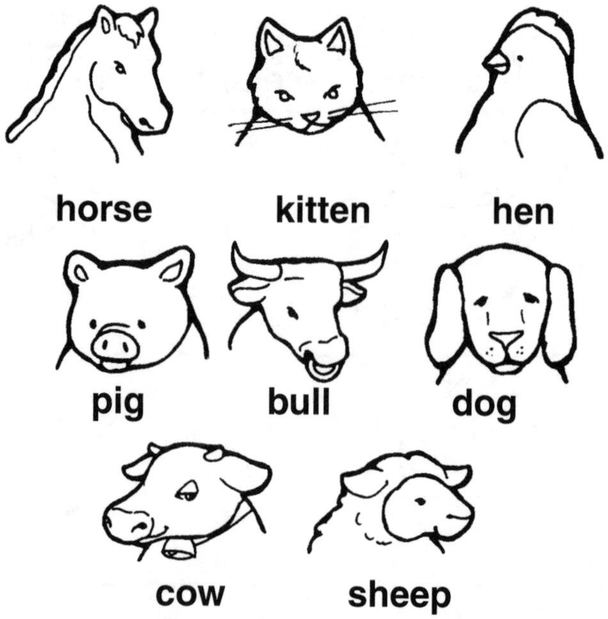
horse
kitten
hen
pig
bull
dog
cow
sheep

Five-a-Day: Skip Counting

Count by 5's.	Count by 5's.	Count by 5's.
5, 10, _____ , 20, _____	30, _____ , 40, _____ , 50	55, 60, _____ , 70, _____

Count the tally marks. (Each bundle is worth 5.) ⑅⑅⑅ ⑅⑅⑅ ⑅⑅⑅ ||| _____ tally marks in all.	Count the tally marks. (Each bundle is worth 5.) ⑅⑅⑅ ⑅⑅⑅ ⑅⑅⑅ ⑅⑅⑅ _____ tally marks in all.

Sentence-a-Day

he   farm   is   near   kraft   school

_____

- -

_____

Write the correct word to complete each phrase.

| bunch | bushel | ear | basket | stalk | wedge |

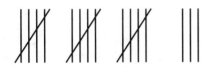

a _____ of grapes   a _____ of celery   a _____ of berries

an _____ of corn   a _____ of apples   a _____ of cheese

Five-a-Day: Skip Counting

Count by 2's.	Count by 2's.	Count by 2's.
2, 4, ___ , 8, 10, ___	14, ___ , ___ , 20, 22	24, ___ , 28, ___ , 32

Count the pairs of gloves. Write the number of gloves under each pair.	Count the wheels on each bike. Write the number of wheels under each bike.
  ___ ___ ___ ___	 ___ ___ ___ ___

Sentence-a-Day

is   molly   and   polly   twins

_____

- -

_____

December						
Sunday	Monday	Tuesday	Wednesday	Thursday	Friday	Saturday
				1	2	3
4	5	6	7	8	9	10
11	12	13	14	15	16	17
18	19	20	21	22	23	24
25	26	27	28	29	30	31

1. What is the name of this month? _____

2. How many days are in this month? _____

3. What is the date of Christmas? _____

4. On what day of the week is December 15? _____

5. On what day does your winter break begin? _____

Five-a-Day: Ordinals

Count across the rows. Circle the 3rd star.	Count across the rows. Circle the 6th snowflake.	Count across the rows. Circle the 8th mitten.

Count across the rows. Circle the 1st and 10th stars.	Count across the rows. Circle the 2nd and 9th heart.

Sentence-a-Day

they   doesn't   look   alike

_____

- -

_____

Where would you most likely find each animal? Write each animal's name under the correct heading.

Forest Animals

1._____

2._____

3._____

4._____

Ocean Animals

1._____

2._____

3._____

4._____

bear   starfish   deer   dolphin   eagle   beaver   lobster   whale

Five-a-Day: Comparing Numbers

Use > and <.	Use > and <.	Use > and <.
22 ◯ 15	19 ◯ 14	18 ◯ 13
_____ is greater than _____ .	_____ is greater than _____ .	_____ is greater than _____ .

Write the number that is greater than 12 and less than 14.	Write the number that is greater than 20 and less than 22.
_____	_____

Sentence-a-Day

do   i   needs   to   eat   my   vegetables

- -

Find each of the hidden words. Color in each word.

V	A	P	P	L	E	S	A	J	C
O	R	A	N	G	E	S	R	B	A
W	A	T	E	R	M	E	L	O	N
G	R	A	P	E	S	X	H	H	P
R	P	U	M	P	K	I	N	S	V
S	M	F	L	E	T	T	U	C	E
T	P	L	U	M	S	M	L	Y	T
C	C	E	L	E	R	Y	P	K	T
P	O	J	D	F	C	O	R	N	L
U	N	C	A	R	R	O	T	S	Z

1. apples
2. carrots
3. celery
4. corn
5. grapes
6. lettuce
7. oranges
8. plums
9. pumpkins
10. watermelon

Five-a-Day: Measurement

Do you weigh more or less than the object?	Do you weigh more or less than the object?	Do you weigh more or less than the object?

more less	more less	more less

Draw something that weighs more than you do.	Draw something that weighs less than you do.

Sentence-a-Day

nurse   richards   say   i   do

_____

- -

_____

A contraction is a short way of writing or saying two words. Read each pair of words and draw a line matching the word to its contraction.

I am	**I'll**
I will	**he's**
he is	**I'm**
he will	**he'll**
she is	**she's**

Five-a-Day: Measurement

Are you taller or shorter than a giraffe?  taller shorter	Are you taller or shorter than a baby?  taller shorter	Are you taller or shorter than your desk? taller shorter

Draw something that is taller than you.	Draw something that is shorter than you.

Sentence-a-Day

what   are   indian   corn

A contraction is a short way of writing 2 words. Read each pair of words and draw a line matching the word to its contraction.

does not	**she'll**
is not	**we'll**
have not	**isn't**
she will	**doesn't**
we will	**haven't**

Five-a-Day: Time

| Write the time.  _____ o'clock | Write the time.  _____ o'clock | Write the time.  _____ o'clock |

| Draw the hands on the clock to show the time that you get up each day.  | Draw the hands on the clock to show the time that you go to sleep.  |

Sentence-a-Day

i   doesn't   know

_____

- -

_____

A contraction is a short way of writing or saying two words. Read each pair of words and draw a line matching the word to its contraction.

could not	they'll
will not	they're
were not	won't
they are	couldn't
they will	weren't

Five-a-Day: Time

Draw both hands.	Draw both hands.	Draw both hands.
 6 o'clock	 9 o'clock	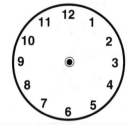 3 o'clock

Draw the hands on the clock to show the time that you go to school.	Draw the hands on the clock to show the time that you eat lunch.

Sentence-a-Day

is   there   many   kinds   of   corn

Find the hidden words. Color in each word as you find it.

M	A	R	C	H	A	P	R	I	L
M	A	Y	O	C	T	O	B	E	R
R	Z	J	U	N	E	I	O	H	E
C	W	D	E	C	E	M	B	E	R
W	J	U	L	Y	T	E	I	C	B
J	A	N	U	A	R	Y	Q	V	O
L	K	A	U	G	U	S	T	H	M
S	E	P	T	E	M	B	E	R	N
N	O	V	E	M	B	E	R	D	I
F	E	B	R	U	A	R	Y	T	I

January
February
March
April
May
June
July
August
September
October
November
December

Name _____

Five-a-Day: Money

Write the number of cents.	Write the number of cents.	Write the number of cents.
_____ ¢	_____ ¢	_____ ¢

Xavier found 6¢ in his shirt pocket and 3¢ in his jacket pocket. How much money did Xavier find in all? Xavier found _____ ¢ in all.	Maria had 5¢ in her piggy bank and 3¢ in her purse. How much money did Maria have in all? Maria has _____ ¢ in all.

Sentence-a-Day

how   much   are   a   penny   worth

_____

- -

_____

An abbreviation is a short way of writing a longer word. Look at the names of the months of the year. Draw a line matching each month to its abbreviation.

January	June	July	Dec.
February	May	August	Sept.
March	Jan.	September	July
April	Apr.	October	Nov.
May	Feb.	November	Aug.
June	Mar.	December	Oct.

Five-a-Day: Money

Write the number of cents.	Write the number of cents.	Write the number of cents.
_____ ¢	_____ ¢	_____ ¢

I have 2 coins that make exactly 6¢. One of the coins is a nickel. What is the other coin?	I have 2 coins that make exactly 10¢. Both of the coins are the same. What are the 2 coins that I have?
_____	_____

Sentence-a-Day

me   thinks   its   worth   it

_____

- -

_____

Write each month's abbreviation.

January	_____	July	_____
February	_____	August	_____
March	_____	September	_____
April	_____	October	_____
May	_____	November	_____
June	_____	December	_____

Five-a-Day: Money

Write the number of cents.	Write the number of cents.	Write the number of cents.
_____ ¢	_____ ¢	_____ ¢

Ashley has a quarter and a nickel in her pocket. How much money does she have in all? Ashley has_____ ¢ in all.	Vincent had 35¢. He spent 10¢ buying a comic book. How much money does Vincent have left? Vincent has _____ ¢ left.

Sentence-a-Day

me   and   my   friend   we   go   to   the   park   yesterday.

_____

- -

_____

The months of the year were scrambled up. Put them back in the correct order using the numbers 1–12.

April	_____	**November**	_____
October	_____	**January**	_____
February	_____	**December**	_____
June	_____	**May**	_____
March	_____	**September**	_____
August	_____	**July**	_____

Five-a-Day: Money

Add.	Add.	Add.
15¢ + 3¢	10¢ + 10¢	5¢ + 3¢

Wesley borrowed 8¢ from his mom and 10¢ from his dad. How much money did Wesley borrow in all?

Wesley borrowed _____¢ in all.

Veronica lent one friend 5¢ and another friend 13¢. How much money did Veronica lend in all?

Veronica lent _____¢ in all.

Sentence-a-Day

us   deposited   our   allowances

Put the months of the year in alphabetical order.

January February March	April May June	July August September	October November December

1. _____

2. _____

3. _____

4. _____

5. _____

6. _____

7. _____

8. _____

9. _____

10. _____

11. _____

12. _____

Five-a-Day: Money

Subtract.	Subtract.	Subtract.
17¢ − 10¢	25¢ − 13¢	13¢ − 11¢

Stephanie had 18¢. She spent 10¢ on an ice cream cone. How much money does Stephanie have left?	Tyrone had 36¢. He bought a model car for 25¢. How much money does Tyrone have left?
Stephanie has _____ ¢ left.	Tyrone has _____ ¢ left.

Sentence-a-Day

i and   jasmine   likes   to   save   our   money

_____

- -

_____

Find each hidden word. Color in the word.

Q	N	I	C	K	E	L	P	L	M
P	Q	W	V	D	O	L	L	A	R
Q	D	I	M	E	S	P	E	N	D
S	O	J	C	E	N	T	S	E	T
O	X	G	E	P	S	P	J	M	C
T	P	Q	R	U	D	O	W	X	P
S	B	P	E	N	N	Y	R	Z	I
Q	U	A	R	T	E	R	O	H	E
C	W	W	C	H	A	N	G	E	T
E	M	O	N	E	Y	S	A	V	E

1. cents
2. change
3. dime
4. dollar
5. money
6. nickel
7. penny
8. quarter
9. save
10. spend

Five-a-Day: Money

Write the number of cents. 	Write the number of cents. 	Write the number of cents. 
_____ ¢	_____ ¢	_____ ¢

Imani had a dime and 2 nickels. How much money did she have in all? Imani had _____ ¢ in all.	Esperanza had 2 quarters and 1 penny. How much money did she have in all? Esperanza had _____ ¢ in all.

Sentence-a-Day

me   mom   and   dad   save   they   money,   too

_____

- -

A compound word is made up of two smaller words.

For example: star + fish = starfish.

Read each pair of words and draw a line to the correct picture of the compound word.

rain + bow =

grand + mother =

fire + fighter =

foot + ball =

tooth + brush =

cup + cake =

Five-a-Day: Money

Write the number of cents.  _____ ¢	Write the number of cents. _____ ¢	Write the number of cents. _____ ¢

Imogene had 3 dimes. How much money does she have? Does she have enough to buy a 25¢ doll? Imogene has _____ ¢ . Yes No	Franklin has a quarter, a dime, and a penny. How much money does he have in all? Does he have enough to buy a 50¢ cookie? Franklin has _____ ¢ . Yes No

Sentence-a-Day

they   go   to   the   bank   of   fresno

- -

A compound word is made up of two smaller words.

For example: star + fish = starfish.

Read each pair of words and draw a line to the correct picture of the compound word.

ginger + bread =

rain + forest =

jelly + fish =

star + fish =

cheese + burger =

Five-a-Day: Money

Write the number of cents.  _____ ¢	Write the number of cents. 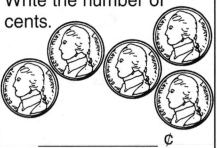 _____ ¢	Write the number of cents. 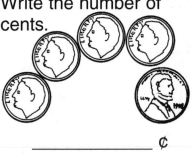 _____ ¢

I have one quarter. How many nickels does it take to make one quarter? It takes _____ nickels to make one quarter.	I have one quarter. How many pennies does it take to make one quarter? It takes _____ pennies to make one quarter.

Sentence-a-Day

the   bank   it   is   on   blackstone   avenue

_____

- -

A compound word is made up of 2 smaller words.

For example: star + fish = starfish.

Read each pair of words and draw a line to the correct picture of the compound word.

type + writer =

sail + boat =

clown + fish =

sea + shell =

candle + light =

basket + ball =

Name _____

Five-a-Day: Measurement

Circle the shortest line.	Circle the shortest line.	Circle the shortest line.

Use counters to measure the length of your paper.	Use counters to measure the length of your pencil.
My paper is _____ counters long.	My pencil is _____ counters long.

Sentence-a-Day

is   neil   the   shortest   boy   at   kratt   school

_____

- -

Complete each sentence with the correct compound word.

> lipstick   butterfly   tablecloth   grasshoppers   cupboard

1. Mr. Thompson put the _____ on the dinner table.

2. Antoinette put on her mother's _____ .

3. Simon opened the _____ to find that it was empty.

4. Deandre likes to collect _____ for his insect collection.

5. A monarch _____ is orange and black.

Five-a-Day: Measurement

Circle the longest line.	Circle the longest line.	Circle the longest line.
_____	_____	_____
_____	_____	_____
_____	_____	_____

Use counters to measure the length of your eraser.	Use counters to measure the length of your crayon.
My eraser is _____ counters long.	My crayon is _____ counters long.

Sentence-a-Day

who   are   the   tallest   person   at   kratt   school

_____

- -

Complete each sentence with the correct compound word.

newspaper   grandmother   mailbox   doorbell   raincoat

1. My _____ came over to visit.

2. Phil went next door and rang the _____ one time.

3. Shane threw the _____ on the front porch.

4. Samantha dropped the letters in the _____ .

5. Donald carried an umbrella and wore a _____ .

Five-a-Day: Place Value

Circle the answer.	Circle the answer.	Circle the answer.
$3 + 1 =$ _____	$6 + 3 =$ _____	$6 - 4 =$ _____
1 2 3 4	4 6 8 9	2 3 4 5

Count by two's to 12. Finish writing the numbers below.	Count by five's to 50. Finish writing the numbers below.
0, _____ , _____ , _____ , _____ , _____ , _____	0, _____ , _____ , _____ , _____ , _____ , _____ , _____ , _____ , _____ , _____

Sentence-a-Day

do   sergio   knows   how   to   count   by   two's

_____

- -

_____

Make compound words using the words in List A and the words in List B. Draw a line from the first part of the compound word in List A to the second part of the compound word in List B.

List A	**List B**
base	fish
cat	brush
tooth	ball
milk	room
bed	shake

Five-a-Day: Place Value

Write a number that is more than 10.	Write a number that is less than 30.	Write a number that is between 25 and 50.
_____	_____	_____

Write the numbers in order from smallest to greatest.	Write the numbers in order from smallest to greatest.
15 11 13 12 14	20 16 19 17 18
____ , ____ , ____ , ____ , ____ ,	____ , ____ , ____ , ____ , ____ ,

Sentence-a-Day

ms.   fishburn   she   like   numbers

_____

- -

Make compound words using the words in List A and the words in List B.
Draw a line from the first part of the compound word in List A to the second
part of the compound word in List B.

List A	**List B**
rubber	shelf
birth	melon
pan	cake
water	day
book	band

Five-a-Day: Place Value

Add.	Add.	Add.
41 + 24	84 + 15	37 + 12

Frank bought 10 tickets. A friend gave him 15 more. How many tickets does Frank have in all?	Mr. Simons caught 30 fish in the morning and 40 fish in the afternoon. How many fish did he catch in all?
Frank has _____ tickets in all.	Mr. Simon caught _____ fish in all.

Sentence-a-Day

what   kinds   of   tickets   is   they

_____

- -

January

Sunday	Monday	Tuesday	Wednesday	Thursday	Friday	Saturday
	1	2	3	4	5	6
7	8	9	10	11	12	13
14	15	16	17	18	19	20
21	22	23	24	25	26	27
28	29	30	31			

1. What is the name of this month?

   _____

2. On what day is the new year? _____

3. What is the date of New Year's Day?

   _____

4. How many days are in this month?

   _____

5. What is your New Year's resolution?

   _____

Five-a-Day: Place Value

Add.	Add.	Add.
34 + 13	56 + 22	41 + 5

Shannon made 4 baskets in the first game and 20 baskets in the second game. How many baskets did Shannon make in all?

Shannon made _____ baskets in all.

Dean had a tie with 31 red dots and 42 blue dots. How many dots in all did Dean have on his tie?

Dean had _____ dots in all.

Sentence-a-Day

me   and   burt   read   seven   books

_____

- -

Use the words in the word bank to complete each sentence.

magazines   library   books   special   information   home

A librarian works in a _____ . A library is a place that is filled

with _____ . People can go to the library to read

_____ , to find _____ on a certain topic and check

out a book to take _____ . Libraries are _____ places!

Five-a-Day: Place Value

Add.	Add.	Add.
24 + 10	66 + 32	74 + 12

Maria had 45 stamps in her collection. Her aunt gave her 54 more. How many stamps does Maria have in all?

Maria has _____ stamps in all.

Ferdinand planted 60 yellow tulips and 10 pink tulips. How many tulips did Ferdinand plant in all?

Ferdinand planted _____ tulips in all.

Sentence-a-Day

gracie   and   heather   they   like   stamps,   too

- -

Use the words in the word bank to complete each sentence.

bandages   shot   hospital   sick   better   medicine

A nurse works in a _____ . Nurses help take care of

_____ or injured people. A nurse will make sure you take your

_____ . He or she will change your _____ . A nurse

might even give you a _____ . Nurses

do all of this because they want you to get _____ .

Five-a-Day: Place Value

Add.	Add.	Add.
22 + 10 _____	24 + 5 _____	32 + 25 _____

Mickey has 70 baseball cards and 20 football cards. How many cards does Mickey have in all? Mickey has _____ cards in all.	My first cookie had 5 chocolate chips in it. My second cookie had 21 chocolate chips in it. How many chocolate chips were there in all? There were _____ chips in all.

Sentence-a-Day

can   you   see   the   ducks   in   the   pond

- -

Use the words in the word bank to complete each sentence.

> **postcards   mail   packages   letters   magazines   raining**

Mail carriers deliver the _____ . They deliver_____ ,

_____ , _____ , and _____ six days a

week. Even if it is _____ , the mail carrier still does the job!

Name _____

Five-a-Day: Place Value

Add.	Add.	Add.
30 + 40 _____	31 + 14 _____	15 + 11 _____

Lisa is 6 years old. Her great grandma is 73 years old. What is the combined total age of Lisa and her grandmother?

They are _____ years old in all.

Kareem's cat is 13 inches tall and Tim's dog is 26 inches tall. How many inches tall are they in all?

They are _____ inches tall in all.

Sentence-a-Day

cant   you   find   the   movie   the   snowman

Use the words in the word bank to complete each sentence.

(songs   read   girls   school   stories   math   boys   write)

A teacher goes to _____ every day. She helps the boys and

girls learn to _____ , _____ , and do

_____ . She reads _____ to the students. She

teaches them new _____ . A teacher loves being

around _____ and _____ .

Five-a-Day: Place Value

Add.	Add.	Add.
40 + 5 _____	32 + 24 _____	47 + 12 _____

Buster looked in his toy box and found 87 cat eye marbles and 10 clear marbles. How many marbles did he find in all? Buster found _____ marbles in all.	Mohammad has 15 pairs of black socks and 23 pairs of white socks. How many pairs of socks does he have in all? Mohammad has _____ pairs of socks.

Sentence-a-Day

me   looked   everywhere   for   it

_____

- -

_____

Use the words in the word bank to complete each sentence.

money   president   place   countries   country

The _____ of the United States has a very important job. The

president runs our _____ . The president makes decisions

about how to spend _____ . The president travels to other

_____ to meet with other leaders. The president

tries to make our country a better _____ to live.

Five-a-Day: Place Value

Add.	Add.	Add.
61 + 3 _____	40 + 14 _____	30 + 9 _____

The students made 55 blueberry pancakes and 41 buttermilk pancakes. How many pancakes did they make in all? They made _____ pancakes in all.	Becky is 3 years old. Her dad is 41 years old. If you added their ages together, how old would they be? They would be _____ years old.

Sentence-a-Day

della   she   like   blueberries

_____

- -

_____

Use the words in the word bank to complete each sentence.

| jobs   message   computer   alphabet   rings   type |

A secretary does many _____ every day. When the phone

_____ , he answers it. Sometimes, he writes down a

_____ . A secretary needs to know how to _____

and how to use a _____ . A secretary also needs to know the

letters of the _____ so he can file any papers.

Five-a-Day: Place Value

Add.	Add.	Add.
82 + 12 _____	94 + 3 _____	25 + 24 _____

My cousin has 63 coins in his piggy bank. I have 21 coins in my piggy bank. How many coins do we have in all?

We have _____ coins in all.

At the pie-eating contest, Leslie ate 41 and Jerome's team ate 38 pies. How many pies did they eat in all?

They ate _____ pies in all.

Sentence-a-Day

she   drawed   we   a   picture   of   worms

_____

- -

_____

Use the words in the word bank to complete each sentence.

carpenter   nails   ladder   toolbelt   hammer

A _____ helps build homes, offices, and stores. A carpenter

uses a _____ . In his toolbelt, the carpenter carries a

_____ and some _____ . Sometimes a

carpenter has to climb a _____ to reach the top of a building.

Carpenters work very hard. Would you like to be a carpenter?

Five-a-Day: Place Value

Subtract.	Subtract.	Subtract.
25 − 11 _____	48 − 32 _____	50 − 20 _____

Derek had 61 balloons. If 10 of the balloons popped, how many balloons does Derek have left? Derek has _____ balloons left.	My sister Cheryl is 27 years old. I am 15 years old. How many years older is Cheryl? Cheryl is ____ years older than I am.

Sentence-a-Day

javier   he   want   a   balloon

_____

- -

_____

Use the words in the word bank to complete each sentence.

drains   water   wrench   leaky   faucets   heads

A plumber works around a lot of _____ . A plumber fixes _____

pipes and unclogs _____ . A plumber can put in new

_____ and new shower _____ .

A plumber always carries a _____ .

Five-a-Day: Place Value

Subtract.	Subtract.	Subtract.
54 − 12 _____	88 − 11 _____	76 − 15 _____

There are 99 days in winter. If 15 days have passed, how many more days of winter are there? There are _____ days of winter left.	Lupe needs 47 candles. There are only 3 candles on the line. How many more candles does Lupe need? Lupe needs _____ more candles.

Sentence-a-Day

when   can   us   go   to   disneyland

_____

- -

_____

Use the words in the word bank to complete each sentence.

(masks   dangerous   pants   burning   equipment   save   coats   hats)

Firefighters have very _____ jobs. Firefighters go into _____

buildings to _____ people's lives. Firefighters wear special _____.

They wear heavy _____ and _____ . They wear

hard _____ . They also wear special breathing _____ .

Five-a-Day: Place Value

Subtract.	Subtract.	Subtract.
46 − 42 _____	38 − 5 _____	89 − 18 _____

There were 64 jelly beans in the jar. Now there are only 22 jelly beans. How many jelly beans are missing? There are _____ jelly beans missing.	Mary Kaye invited 99 people to the party. Only 30 came. How many people did not come to the party? _____ people did not come to the party.

Sentence-a-Day

why   didnt   you   came   to   the   party

Use the words in the word bank to complete each sentence.

(brush   washes   dryer   cut   hairdresser   scissors   color)

A _____ cuts hair. First the hairdresser _____ your hair.

Then she might _____ it , give you a permanent, or even

change the _____ of your hair! A hairdresser uses a pair of

_____ , a hair _____, and a hair _____ to do this job.

Five-a-Day: Place Value

Subtract.	Subtract.	Subtract.
58 − 38 _____	44 − 42 _____	95 − 4 _____

Jeremy counted 96 stars on Monday and only 26 on Tuesday. How many fewer stars did Jeremy see on Tuesday than on Monday? Jeremy saw _____ fewer stars.	Leo baked 30 cupcakes for his class. His dog ate 20 of the cupcakes. How many cupcakes does Leo have left? Leo has _____ cupcakes left.

Sentence-a-Day

why   did   leo   name   his   dog   bandit

_____

Use the words in the word bank to complete each sentence.

fictional   author   nonfiction   words

An _____ is someone who writes stories for other people to

read. The author might write a _____ story. A fictional story is

one the author makes up. An author might write a story that is

_____ . Nonfiction means that it is a true story.

A good author needs to know a lot of _____ !

Five-a-Day: Place Value

Subtract.	Subtract.	Subtract.
23¢ − 13¢ ‾‾‾‾‾	42¢ − 12¢ ‾‾‾‾‾	26¢ − 22¢ ‾‾‾‾‾

Joe had 34¢ in his pocket. If 21¢ fell out of the hole in his pocket, how much money does he have left? Joe has _____ left.	Esmeralda had 95¢ in her lunch bag. She gave her friend 14¢. How much money does she have left in her lunch bag? Esmeralda has _____ left in her lunch bag.

Sentence-a-Day

ryan   he   want   to   buy   a   book

_____

- -

_____

Adjectives are words that describe a noun (a person, place, or thing). Draw a line matching the picture with the correct adjective and noun phrase. Color the pictures to match each phrase.

a brown   a yellow   a purple   a green   a red   orange
bear   sun   bow   frog   strawberry   carrots

Five-a-Day: Place Value

Add.	Add.	Add.
30¢ + 20¢ ————	71¢ + 5¢ ————	31¢ + 30¢ ————

Mia spent 55¢ on popcorn and 20¢ for gum. How much money did Mia spend in all? Mia spent _____ in all.	Elvis bought an eraser for 45¢ and a pencil for 20¢. How much money did Elvis spend in all? Elvis spent _____ in all.

Sentence-a-Day

did   you   like   the   new   godzilla   movie

Adjectives are words that describe a noun (a person, place, or thing). Draw a line matching the picture with the correct adjective and noun phrase.

| a warm <br> sweater | a white <br> cloud | a hot <br> fire | a tall <br> ostrich | a tasty <br> pie | a happy <br> snowman |

Five-a-Day: Place Value

Subtract.	Subtract.	Subtract.
45¢ − 13¢ _____	56¢ − 5¢ _____	89¢ − 80¢ _____

Helen earned 75¢ washing the car. She put 50¢ in her bank. How much money does Helen have left? Helen has _____ left.	Val's grandma gave her 95¢. Val spent 50¢ on a pocket folder. How much money does she have left? Val has _____ left.

Sentence-a-Day

what   does   her   feed   the   turtle

_____

- -

_____

Read each sentence. Circle the adjective in each sentence. Draw a line under the noun it modifies in each sentence.

1. The happy girl blew out the candles.

2. The crying man watched the movie.

3. The sleepy baby was in the crib.

4. The hungry woman ate dinner.

5. The laughing boy enjoyed the movie.

Five-a-Day: Place Value

Subtract.	Subtract.	Subtract.
44¢ − 11¢ ————	50¢ − 20¢ ————	93¢ − 32¢ ————

Christine cleaned the pool for 85¢. She bought a pool toy for 73¢. How much money does Christine have left? Christine has _____¢ left.	Mom had 85¢ in her wallet. She spent 50¢ on a carton of juice. How much money does Mom have left? Mom has _____¢ left.

Sentence-a-Day

me   and   hannah   seen   a   silver   dollar

_____

- -

_____

Read each sentence. Write the missing adjective on the line.

> **green   purple   black   yellow   red**

1. The _____ plums were fresh.

2. The _____ lemon tasted sour.

3. The _____ grapes were delicious.

4. The _____ apple was crispy.

5. The _____ raisins were wrinkly.

Five-a-Day: Place Value

Sari spent 29¢ on gum and 30¢ on candy. How much money did she spend in all? _____ ¢	Rob has 25¢. He earned 10¢ more by raking leaves. How much money does Rob have? _____ ¢	Ray has 45¢. He spent 15¢ on a toy. How much money does Ray have left? _____ ¢
Deb has 95¢. She spends 85¢ on a toy for her cat. How much money does Deb have left? Deb has _____ ¢ left.	Bob has 35¢. He put 20¢ into his savings account. How much money does Bob have left? Bob has _____ ¢ left.	

Sentence-a-Day

what   you   gonna   spend   your   money   on

_____

- -

_____

Read each sentence. Write the missing adjective on the line.

beautiful   woolly   prickly   buzzing   chirping

1. The _____ porcupine has lots of quills.

2. The _____ bird sang a song.

3. The _____ sheep slept in the field.

4. The _____ bee flew in the garden.

5. The _____ butterfly was resting on a flower.

Five-a-Day: Place Value

Add.	Subtract.	Subtract.
23 + 14 _____	34 – 12 _____	52 – 1 _____

Hansel has 75 pieces of candy. He gives 35 pieces to Gretel. How many pieces of candy does Hansel have left? He has_____ pieces of candy.	Ivan recycled 14 cans of soda and 25 bundles of newspapers. How many items did Ivan recycle in all? He recycled _____ items.

Sentence-a-Day

me   helped   roger   clean   up   him   room

_____

- -

_____

Look at each picture. Write the beginning and ending sound for each picture.

____ o ____

____ i ____

____ a ____

____ a ____

____ u ____

____ e ____

Five-a-Day: Add and Subtract to 12

Meg has 2 bows. She buys 4 more. How many does she now have?	Dad has 23 ties. He gave away 11 ties. How many ties does Dad now have?	Leanne has 9 birds. If 3 birds fly away, how many birds are left?
____ + ____ = ____	____ − ____ = ____	____ − ____ = ____

Pao has 19 tires. Pao sells 15 of them. How many tires does Pao have left?	Sara has 17 cream pies. She sells 11 of them. How many pies does Sara now have?
Pao has _____ tires left.	Sara now has _____ pies.

Sentence-a-Day

me   and   lee   plays   on   the   computer

_____

- -

Look at each picture. Write the beginning and ending sound for each picture.

____a____

____e____

____e____

____a____

____u____

____o____

Five-a-Day: Add and Subtract to 12

Add.

$3 + 7 =$ _____

Add.

$5 + 5 =$ _____

Add.

$6 + 5 =$ _____

Add.

$2 +$ _____ $= 9$

_____ $+ 2 = 9$

Add.

$3 +$ _____ $= 10$

_____ $+ 3 = 10$

Sentence-a-Day

do   charlotte   has   a   computer

_____

- -

_____

February

Sunday	Monday	Tuesday	Wednesday	Thursday	Friday	Saturday
	1	2	3	4	5	6
7	8	9	10	11	12	13
14	15	16	17	18	19	20
21	22	23	24	25	26	27
28						

1. What is the name of this month?

   _____

2. How many days are in this month? _____

3. What is the day and the date of Valentine's Day?

   _____

4. Name one president whose birthday is in February?

   _____

Five-a-Day: Add and Subtract to 12

Add.	Add.	Add.
4 + 8 = _____	7 + 3 = _____	5 + 6 = _____

Add.	Add.
9 + _____ = 12	5 + _____ = 12
_____ + 9 = 12	_____ + 5 = 12

Sentence-a-Day

us   have   computers   at   school

_____

- -

_____

Write the insects' names in alphabetical order.

fly   mosquito   dragonfly   butterfly

ladybug   locust   bee   ant

1. _____

2. _____

3. _____

4. _____

5. _____

6. _____

7. _____

8. _____

Five-a-Day: Add and Subtract to 12

Add.
 	
  9
+ 3
___
	Add.
	
	  6
	+ 4
	___
		Add.
		
		  8
		+ 3
		___

I made 1 star. My friend Mee made 8 stars. How many stars did we make in all? We made _____ stars in all.	Dareen caught 9 butterflies. Devin caught 3 butterflies. How many butterflies did they catch? They caught _____ butterflies in all.

Sentence-a-Day

why   are   the   sky   black   at   night

_____

Read the scrambled sentence. Write the words in the correct order.

animal   left   What   prints?   these

_____

_____

_____

Five-a-Day: Add and Subtract to 12

Add.	Add.	Add.
5 + 7 ———	4 + 5 ———	9 + 2 ———

Justin made 7 pictures using crayons and 4 pictures using chalk. How many pictures did Justin make in all?	Louisa bought a dozen eggs. If 6 of the eggs broke, how many eggs does Louisa have left?
Justin made _____ pictures in all.	Louisa has _____ eggs left.

Sentence-a-Day

me   helped   louisa   clean   up   the   mess

_____

- -

_____

Answer the questions about eggs.

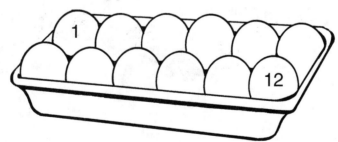

1. How many eggs are in one dozen? _____

2. The first egg is marked. Put an "X" on the second egg to its right.

3. Put a ★ on the third egg.

4. Make a circle around the ninth egg.

5. How many eggs are in a baker's dozen? _____

Five-a-Day: Add and Subtract to 12

Add.	Add.	Add.
4 + 6 = _____	3 + 8 = _____	5 + 6 = _____
6 + 4 = _____	8 + 3 = _____	6 + 5 = _____

Use the numbers 3, 7, and 10 to make two addition problems.	Use the numbers 3, 7, and 10 to make two subtraction problems.
_____ + _____ = 10	10 − _____ = _____
_____ + _____ = 10	10 − _____ = _____

Sentence-a-Day

why   do   abraham   lincoln   wear   a   hat

_____

- -

_____

Look at each picture and its word. Write the missing vowel.
(Vowels are a, e, i, o, and u.)

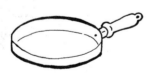

p _____ n

c _____ t

st _____ mp

h _____ nd

pl _____ nt

b _____ t

Five-a-Day: Add and Subtract to 12

Add.	Add.	Add.
5 + 7 = _____	4 + 7 = _____	4 + 8 = _____
7 + 5 = _____	7 + 4 = _____	8 + 4 = _____

Use the numbers 1, 9, and 10 to make two addition problems.	Use the numbers 1, 9, and 10 to make two subtraction problems.
_____ + _____ = 10	10 − _____ = _____
_____ + _____ = 10	10 − _____ = _____

Sentence-a-Day

aint   his   picture   on   a   penny

_____

- -

Look at each picture and its word. Write the missing vowel.
(Vowels are a, e, i, o, and u.)

r ____ st

sl ____ d

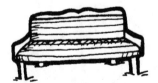

b ____ nch

d ____ sk

h ____ n

____ gg

Five-a-Day: Add and Subtract to 12

Add.	Add.	Add.
2 + 9 = _____	7 + 5 _____	3 + 7 = _____
9 + 2 = _____		7 + 3 = _____

Use the numbers 4, 7, and 11 to make two addition problems.	Use the numbers 4, 7, and 11 to make two subtraction problems.
_____ + _____ = _____ _____ + _____ = _____	_____ − _____ = _____ _____ − _____ = _____

Sentence-a-Day

didnt   you   watch   the   washington   parade

_____

- -

Look at each picture and its word. Write the missing vowel.
(Vowels are a, e, i, o, and u.)

____gloo

m ____ lk

f ____ sh

ch ____ ck

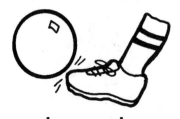

k ____ ck

p ____ n

Five-a-Day: Add and Subtract to 12

Add. Circle the doubles.	Add. Circle the doubles.	Add. Circle the doubles.
2 + 2 = _____	1 + 1 = _____	3 + 3 = _____
6 + 5 = _____	9 + 1 = _____	4 + 4 = _____

Use the numbers 5, 6, and 11 to make two addition problems.	Use the numbers 5, 6, and 11 to make two subtraction problems.
_____ + _____ = _____ _____ + _____ = _____	_____ − _____ = _____ _____ − _____ = _____

Sentence-a-Day

we   goed   to   sacramento   to   see   the   parade

Look at each picture and its word. Write the missing vowel.
(Vowels are a, e, i, o, and u.)

f ___ x

m ___ p

l ___ g

___strich

d ___ ll

g ___ lf ball

Five-a-Day: Add and Subtract to 14

Circle the answer. Pete has 4 rocks. He finds 5 more. How many does he have in all? 9 17	Circle the answer. If 7 mice were sitting and 4 mice ran away how many mice were left? 9 3	Circle the answer. If 11 horses were eating and 3 horses stopped eating how many horses were eating? 12 8

Use the numbers 3, 9, and 12 to make two addition problems. _____ + _____ = _____ _____ + _____ = _____	Use the numbers 3, 9, and 12 to make two subtraction problems. _____ − _____ = _____ _____ − _____ = _____

Sentence-a-Day

cant   you   run   any   faster

_____

- -

Look at each picture and its word. Write the missing vowel.
(Vowels are a, e, i, o, and u.)

sl ___ g

s ___ n

c ___ p

b ___ g

p ___ mp

t ___ b

Five-a-Day: Add and Subtract to 14

Subtract. $\begin{array}{r} 11 \\ -\ 4 \\ \hline \end{array}$	Subtract. $\begin{array}{r} 11 \\ -\ 5 \\ \hline \end{array}$	Subtract. $\begin{array}{r} 10 \\ -\ 9 \\ \hline \end{array}$

Ginger had 9 seashells. Now she has only 2. How many seashells did she lose? Ginger lost _____ seashells.	Rosemary made 11 cookies. Her brother ate some. Now there are only 2 left. How many cookies did her brother eat? He ate _____ cookies.

Sentence-a-Day

rosemary   uses   grandma   nora's   recipe

_____

- -

_____

Look at each picture and its word. Write the missing vowel.
(Vowels are a, e, i, o, and u.)

v ___ t

sl ___ ppers

w ___ b

___ nt

v ___ n

bl ___ cks

Five-a-Day: Add and Subtract to 14

Subtract.	Subtract.	Subtract.
6 − 3 = ____	5 − 1 = ____	12 − 0 = ____
1 − 1 = ____	9 − 2 = ____	12 − 3 = ____

Stacy had 12 pieces of candy. She gave Raul 6 pieces. How many pieces of candy does Stacy have left?	Solomon has 12 pencils. His dog ate 4 of them. How many pencils does Solomon have left?
Stacy has _____ pieces left.	Solomon has _____ pencils left.

Sentence-a-Day

grandma   nora   lives   in   san   francisco

_____

- -

_____

Look at each picture and its word. Write the missing vowel.
(Vowels are a, e, i, o, and u.)

c ___ mp

tw ___ g

s ___ b

h ___ m

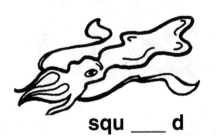

squ ___ d

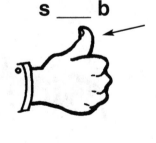

th ___ mb

Five-a-Day: Add and Subtract to 14

Add.	Add.	Subtract.
$1 + 2 + 5 =$ ___	$1 + 2 + 1 + 2 + 1$ $=$ ___	$11 - 4 =$ ___ $11 - 7 =$ ___

Gwen has 10 pigs. If 3 pigs ran into the barn, how many pigs did not run into the barn?	Leo picked 12 blueberries. He gave 9 of them to his friend. How many blueberries does Leo have left?
_____ pigs did not run into the barn.	Leo has _____ blueberries left.

Sentence-a-Day

farmer   aziz   has   much   animals

Look at each picture and its word. Write the missing vowel.
(Vowels are a, e, i, o, and u.)

f ___ n

h ___ t

c ___ n

j ___ r

b ___ g

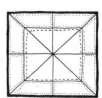

qu ___ lt

Five-a-Day: Add and Subtract to 14

Solve.	Solve.	Solve.
6 + 5 = _____	9 + 1 = _____	7 + 5 = _____
11 – 5 = _____	10 – 1 = _____	12 – 5 = _____

Hope picked 7 strawberries and 3 peaches. How many pieces of fruit did Hope pick in all?	Omari can play 9 songs on his bass. He has already played 3 songs. How many more songs can Omari play?
Hope picked _____ pieces.	Omari can play _____ more songs.

Sentence-a-Day

him   favorite   animal   are   the   cow

_____

- -

A singular noun means that there is only one person, place, or thing. Draw a line to match each picture to its name.

man   goose   child   mouse   woman   person

Five-a-Day: Add and Subtract to 14

Circle the 4th star.	Circle the 7th letter.	Circle the 1st number.
★★★★★★★★★★★	A A A A A A A A A A A	8888888888888888

Farmer Ada had 14 animals. If 8 of them were chickens, how many were not chickens? _____ animals were not chickens.	Farmer Cary feeds the cows 9 bales of hay. He feeds the horses 4 bales of hay. How many more bales of hay does he give to the cows than to the horses? He gives the cows _____ more bales of hay.

Sentence-a-Day

i   likes   the   sheeps   best

_____

- -

_____

A plural noun means that there is more than one person, place, or thing. Draw a line to match each picture to its name.

men   geese   children   mice   women   people

Five-a-Day: Add and Subtract to 14

Hector has 10 oranges. He eats 2. How many are left? ____ – ____ = ____	There are 8 chicks. If 2 run away, how many are left? ____ – ____ = ____	There are 12 owls. If 9 fly away, how many are left? ____ – ____ = ____

Bea made 6 candles. She finds 5 more. How many candles does Bea now have? Bea has _____ candles.	Tim has 9 ducks. If 2 ducks waddle away, how many ducks does Tim have left? Tim has _____ ducks left.

Sentence-a-Day

they   is   so   soft

Look at each picture. Circle the singular noun or plural noun that matches the picture.

child children   **goose geese**   **woman women**

person people   **man men**   **mouse mice**

Five-a-Day: Add and Subtract to 14

Add.	Add.	Subtract.
$\begin{array}{r} 2 \\ +\ 9 \\ \hline \end{array}$	$\begin{array}{r} 5 \\ +\ 5 \\ \hline \end{array}$	$\begin{array}{r} 12 \\ -\ 3 \\ \hline \end{array}$

Manuel made 11 cakes. He sold 6 at the fair. How many cakes does Manuel have left? Manuel has _____ cakes left.	Duaa made 4 pita sandwiches. Then she made 7 more. How many pita sandwiches did Duaa make? Duaa made _____ pita sandwiches.

Sentence-a-Day

me   and   norma   went   to   the   fair

- -

Find each hidden word. Color the word in.

P	E	R	S	O	N	O	L	Q	S
B	M	O	U	S	E	H	G	K	X
S	S	M	I	C	E	X	K	K	X
G	O	O	S	E	G	E	E	S	E
I	K	W	O	M	E	N	O	J	T
T	T	M	A	N	T	D	F	H	R
X	C	H	I	L	D	M	E	N	Q
P	E	O	P	L	E	J	N	C	X
F	N	R	L	R	W	O	M	A	N
C	H	I	L	D	R	E	N	C	C

1. child
2. children
3. goose
4. geese
5. man
6. men
7. mouse
8. mice
9. person
10. people
11. woman
12. women

Five-a-Day: Add and Subtract to 14

Circle the correct answer. $5 + 1 = $ ____ 4 5 6 Not here	Circle the correct answer. $4 - 2 = $ ____ 0 1 2 Not here	Circle the correct answer. $9 - 6 = $ ____ 2 3 4 Not here

Stuart ate 18 candies. Glenn ate 11 candies. How many candies did they eat in all? They ate _____ candies in all.	Taylor counted 8 red roses and 6 white roses in the garden. How many roses did Taylor find in all? Taylor found _____ roses in all.

Sentence-a-Day

me   and   rachel   wanta   pick   the   flowers

_____

- -

_____

Write the beginning blend for each of the words.

cl   cl   cl   dr   dr   dr

___agon   ___apes   ___imb

___ap   ___um   ___ip

Five-a-Day: Add and Subtract to 14

Add.	Add.	Add.
$6 + 8 =$ _____	$9 + 4 =$ _____	$5 + 6 =$ _____

Yvonne collected 6 cans and 7 newspapers to take to the recycling center. How many items did Yvonne collect in all? Yvonne collected _____ items in all.	Lars is 7 years old. Lonnie is 7 years old. If their ages were added together, how old would they be? They would be _____ years old.

Sentence-a-Day

chelsea's   birthday   is   in   march

Write the beginning blend for each of the words.

fl   fl   fl   fr   fr   fr

___ag   ___iend   ___isbee

___ies   ___ood   ___amingo

Five-a-Day: Add and Subtract to 14

Add.	Add.	Add.
6 + 4	8 + 4	1 + 9

Lassie ate 5 dog bones for breakfast and 9 for lunch. How many dog bones did Lassie eat in all?

Lassie ate _____ bones in all.

Sugar Pie barked 8 times at the mail carrier and 3 times at the meter reader. How many times did Sugar Pie bark?

Sugar Pie barked _____ times in all.

Sentence-a-Day

what   does   you   call   your   dog

_____

- -

_____

Write the beginning blend for each of the words.

gl   gl   gl   gr   gr   gr

____ue   ____ade   ____aduate

____ove   ____oup   ____obe

Five-a-Day: Add and Subtract to 14

Add.	Add.	Add.
5 + 5 = _____	6 + 1 = _____	4 + 6 = _____

Max bought 12 pounds of dog food. His dog Heidi ate 6 pounds of it. How many pounds of dog food does Max have left?

Max has _____ pounds left.

The dog had 10 fleas. If 2 fleas jumped off, how many fleas were left?

The dog had _____ fleas left.

Sentence-a-Day

she   name   is   sugar   pie

_____

- -

Write the beginning blend for each of the words.

pl   pl   pl   pr   pr   pr

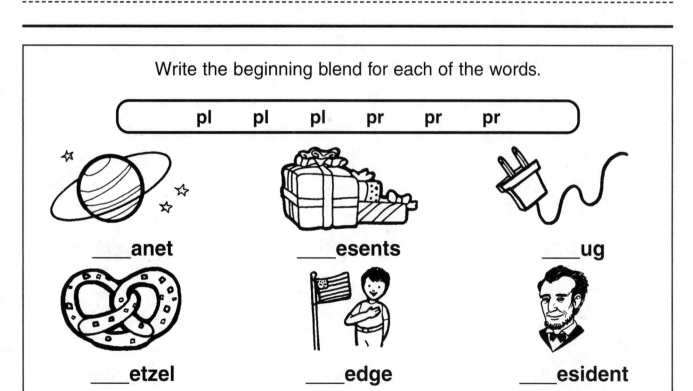

____anet   ____esents   ____ug

____etzel   ____edge   ____esident

Name ______________________________ **Practice 132**

Five-a-Day: Add and Subtract to 18

Add.

7 + 7 = ______

Add.

9 + 6 = ______

Add.

9 + 9 = ______

Liz bought 7 bird toys and 9 dog toys. How many animal toys did Liz buy in all?

Liz bought ________ toys in all.

Ana has 8 yellow fish and 7 silver fish. How many fish does Ana have in all?

Ana has _________ fish in all.

Sentence-a-Day

inga have many tropical fish

Write the beginning blend for each of the words.

sc sc sc sl sl sl

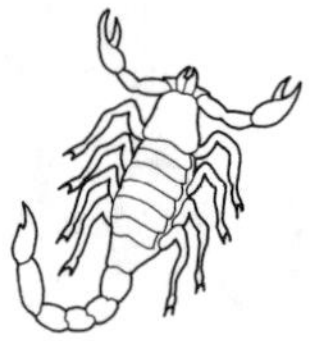

____orpion

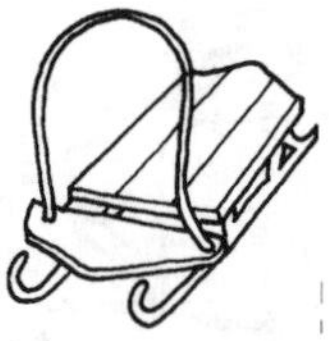

____ed

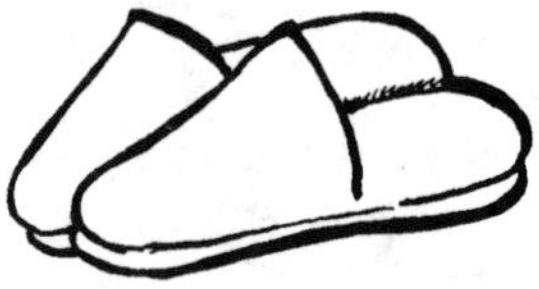

____ippers

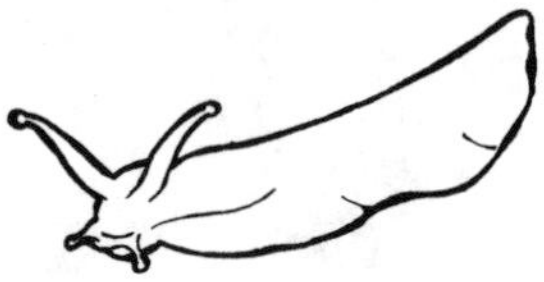

____ug

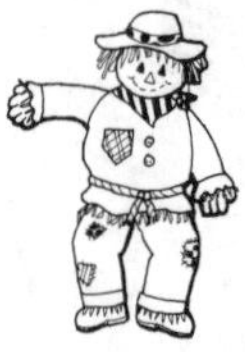

____arecrow

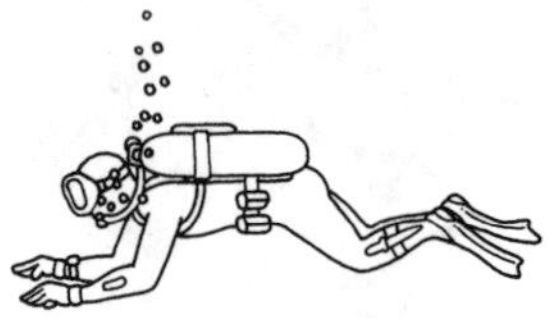

____uba

Five-a-Day: Adding Three Numbers

Add.	Add.	Add.
3 3 + 2 ___	2 1 + 4 ___	4 5 + 1 ___

Jacob has 5 books. Bart has 3 books. Amy has 2 books. How many books do they have in all? They have _____ books in all.	The recipe calls for 1 cup of flour, 5 cups of sugar, and 1 cup of milk. How many cups of ingredients do I need to use? I need to use _____ cups.

Sentence-a-Day

me   and   ira   is   gonna   make   a   pie

_____

- -

Write the beginning blend for each of the words.

> sm   sm   sn   sn   sn   sn

___ake

___ile

___ell

___eakers

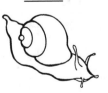
___ail

___owman

Five-a-Day: Adding Three Numbers

Add.	Add.	Add.
3 1 + 0 _____	3 5 + 4 _____	2 2 + 2 _____

Brittany collected 6 grasshoppers, 2 ladybugs, and 3 butterflies. How many insects did Brittany collect in all?	There were 8 crows, 1 bluebird, and 1 robin sitting in a tree. How many birds were there in all?
Brittany collected _____ insects.	There were _____ birds in all.

Sentence-a-Day

ladybugs   they   are   red   and   black

_____

- -

_____

Find each of the hidden words. Color the word in.

D	R	A	G	O	N	F	L	Y	R
L	O	C	U	S	T	F	L	Y	V
S	B	E	E	M	F	T	M	L	Y
C	R	I	C	K	E	T	T	C	P
K	B	U	T	T	E	R	F	L	Y
T	P	O	A	N	T	J	D	F	L
U	N	Z	T	I	E	R	M	B	S
N	D	Y	D	X	S	H	L	B	Z
M	O	S	Q	U	I	T	O	R	D
W	L	A	D	Y	B	U	G	V	P

1. ant
2. bee
3. butterfly
4. cricket
5. dragonfly
6. fly
7. ladybug
8. locust
9. mosquito

Five-a-Day: Adding Three Numbers

Add.	Add.	Add.
14 13 + 11	14 11 + 10	21 13 + 12

Cross out the number that is not needed to solve the problem.	13 12 + 53 _____ 25	Cross out the number that is not needed to solve the problem.	44 44 + 10 _____ 88

Sentence-a-Day

uncle   raymond   collect   grasshoppers

_____

- -

_____

Insects

Insects and spiders are not in the same animal group. Insects have 3 body parts and 6 legs. Spiders have 2 body parts and 8 legs.

Insects come in many different colors. For example, butterflies, like the monarch, can be very brightly colored. Insects can also crawl, walk, or fly.

Some insects can be very helpful. The ladybug's favorite food is aphids. One ladybug can eat many aphids in one day. Ladybugs are not only pretty, but they help keep plants healthy!

1. How many legs do all insects have? _____

2. How many body parts do all insects have? _____

3. Are spiders insects? Why or why not? _____

Five-a-Day: Adding Three Numbers

Add.
 	
  41
  30
+ 12
———
	Add.
	
	  24
	  23
	+ 22
	———
		Add.
		
		  51
		  24
		+ 11
		———

Cross out the number that is not needed to solve the problem.
 	
  42
  33
+ 14
———
  47
		Cross out the number that is not needed to solve the problem.
		
		  36
		  20
		+ 11
		———
		  56

Sentence-a-Day

cyril   he   has   lots   of   caterpillars

Color in only the insects.

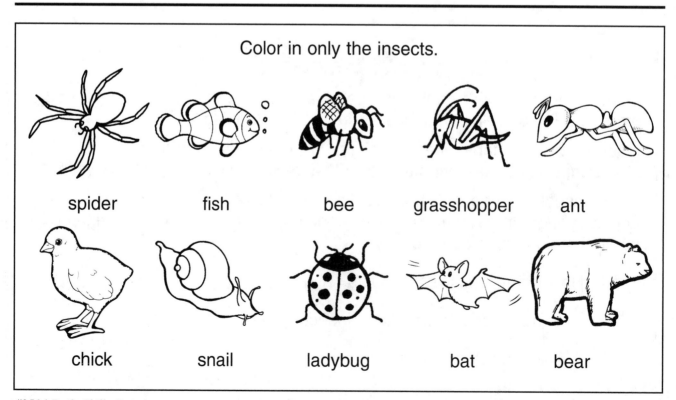

spider   fish   bee   grasshopper   ant

chick   snail   ladybug   bat   bear

Five-a-Day: Add and Subtract to 18

Subtract.	Subtract.	Subtract.
$13 - 9 =$ _____	$12 - 9 =$ _____	$14 - 9 =$ _____

Cecil had 13 butterflies. If 8 of them flew away, how many butterflies does Cecil have left?	Kenya found 10 snails in her garden. She picked up 5 of them. How many snails are left in Kenya's garden?
Cecil has _____ butterflies left.	Kenya has _____ snails left.

Sentence-a-Day

sophie   have   much   flowers   in   her   yard

_____

- -

March						
Sunday	Monday	Tuesday	Wednesday	Thursday	Friday	Saturday
	1	2	3	4	5	6
7	8	9	10	11	12	13
14	15	16	17	18	19	20
21	22	23	24	25	26	27
28	29	30	31			

1. What is the name of this month?

_____

2. How many days are in the month of March? _____

3. On what day of the week does March begin? _____

4. On what day of the week does March end? _____

5. How many odd days are there in March? _____

6. Are there more Tuesdays or Fridays?

_____

Five-a-Day: Add and Subtract to 18

Subtract.	Subtract.	Subtract.
$11 - 6 =$ _____	$14 - 5 =$ _____	$14 - 8 =$ _____

Cory planted 13 carrot seeds. Only 5 sprouted. How many carrot seeds did not sprout? _____ carrot seeds did not sprout.	Raven planted 12 squash seeds and 6 tomato seeds. How many seeds did she plant in all? Raven planted _____ seeds in all.

Sentence-a-Day

cans   we   plant   some   herbs

_____

- -

_____

Write the beginning blend for each of the words.

sk   sk   sk   sp   sp   sp

___ydiving   ___unk   ___oon

___aghetti   ___arkler   ___eleton

Five-a-Day: Add and Subtract to 18

Subtract.	Subtract.	Subtract.
15 − 8 = ____	14 − 7 = ____	16 − 7 = ____

Mr. Clover picked 16 heads of lettuce. He gave us 9 heads of lettuce. How many heads of lettuce does Mr. Clover have left? Mr. Clover has _____ heads of lettuce left.	Mrs. Peabody picked 15 ears of corn. If 6 of the ears had bugs, how many ears did not have bugs? _____ ears did not have bugs.

Sentence-a-Day

me   and   uncle   jesse   have   some   herb   seeds

_____

- -

_____

Write the beginning blend for each of the words.

| st | st | st | sw | sw | sw |

____age

____an

____ing

____ordfish

____amp

____apler

Name _____

Five-a-Day: Add and Subtract to 18

Subtract.	Subtract.	Subtract.
17 − 8 _____	16 − 7 _____	13 − 5 _____

Ms. Smith put 15 vegetables into her pot of soup. If 7 of the vegetables were onions, how many were not onions? _____ were not onions.	Mr. Wimple planted 18 radish seeds. The birds ate 8 of the seeds. How many radish seeds are left? There are _____ radish seeds left.

Sentence-a-Day

do   mr.   young   likes   to   work   in   his   garden

_____

Write the beginning blend for each of the words.

tr	tr	tr	tw	tw	tw

___enty

___ap

___iceratops

___ain

___ins

___elve

144

Five-a-Day: Add and Subtract to 18

Add.	Subtract.	Solve.
9 + 6 = _____	15 − 9 = _____	9 + _____ = 15
6 + 9 = _____	15 − 6 = _____	6 + _____ = 15

A group of Girl Scouts went camping. If 13 of the girls set up camp while 9 went on a hike, how many Girl Scouts were there in all? There were _____ Girl Scouts in all.	Eight Boy Scouts were busy cooking dinner. The rest were setting up the tents. There were 14 Boy Scouts in all. How many were setting up the tents? _____ Boy Scouts were setting up the tents.

Sentence-a-Day

my   dad   was   an   eagle   scout

_____

- -

Write the correct word on the line beneath each picture.

canoe   lantern   oar   pole   stars   tent

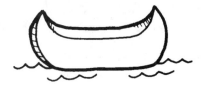

_____   _____   _____

_____   _____   _____

Name _____

Five-a-Day: Add and Subtract to 18

Subtract.	Subtract.	Subtract.
15 – 7 = _____	14 – 7 = _____	13 – 8 = _____

Dave picked up 8 blue oars and 9 gold oars. How many oars did Dave pick up in all? Dave picked up _____ oars in all.	Hilda gathered 6 small twigs and 9 large twigs to build a camp fire. How many twigs in all did Hilda gather? Hilda gathered _____ twigs in all.

Sentence-a-Day

myra   have   earned   twelve   badges

Read each riddle. Write the answer on the line.

tent   tree   fish   marshmallow

I am white and soft. I can be roasted on a stick. What am I?

a _____

I am silver. I swim in the water. I have gills. What am I?

a _____

I am green. I smell nice. I have prickly needles. What am I?

a _____

I am made of material. I sit on the ground. I have a zipper. What am I?

a _____

Five-a-Day: Add and Subtract to 18

Subtract.	Subtract.	Subtract.
$18 - 9 =$ _____	$16 - 9 =$ _____	$18 - 8 =$ _____

The Blue Troop was painting rocks. If 2 of the 18 members were painting rocks, how many members were not painting rocks? _____ were not painting rocks.	Nine of the Red Troop members were making belts. Five of the Orange Troop members were making belts, too. How many members were making belts? _____ were making belts.

Sentence-a-Day

tyra   she   are   working   on   her   safety   skills

_____

- -

_____

Find each hidden word. Color the word in.

C	A	M	P	C	A	N	O	E	H
S	T	I	C	K	P	R	V	S	M
F	F	O	R	E	S	T	T	M	L
L	A	N	T	E	R	N	Y	T	C
P	K	T	P	O	J	D	F	L	U
N	Z	T	F	I	S	H	I	N	G
I	E	R	M	B	S	N	D	Y	D
X	F	I	R	E	S	H	L	B	Z
C	R	A	F	T	S	T	E	N	T
R	T	R	O	O	P	D	W	V	P

1. camp
2. canoe
3. crafts
4. fishing
5. fire
6. forest
7. lantern
8. stick
9. tent
10. troop

Name _____

Five-a-Day: Add and Subtract to 18

Solve.	Solve.	Solve.
7 + _____ = 7	3 + _____ = 7	2 + _____ = 10
0 + _____ = 7	4 + _____ = 7	8 + _____ = 10

The scouts were roasting marshmallows. They burned 3 of the 18 marshmallows. How many marshmallows did not burn? _____ marshmallows did not burn.	At the crafts station, 6 scouts made bracelets and 8 made hats. How many crafts were made in all? There were _____ crafts made in all.

Sentence-a-Day

tyson   he   catched   3   fish

_____

- -

_____

Use the words in the word bank to label the parts of a campsite.

Word Bank

fire

forest

logs

moon

owl

tent

tracks

Five-a-Day: Add and Subtract to 18

Add.	Add.	Add.
9 + 8 ____	8 + 9 ____	9 + 6 ____

The scouts spotted 5 bears and 9 cougars. How many animals did they see?	One of the scouts sold 7 boxes of cookies on Monday and 6 boxes of cookies on Tuesday. How many boxes did she sell in all?
The scouts saw _____ animals.	She sold _____ boxes in all.

Sentence-a-Day

how   did   desiree   earns   her   badges

_____

- -

_____

Complete each sentence using the words in the word bank.

| marshmallows   tree   camping   tent   fire   sticks   yummy |

My family and I went _____ .

I put up my own _____ .

My tent was by a big _____ .

At night, we made a _____ .

We put _____ on

_____ and roasted them.

They were _____ !

Five-a-Day: Geometry, Patterns, and Shapes

Draw a square.	Draw a circle.	Draw a triangle.

Look at the triangle below. How many triangles do you see?	Look at the square below. How many squares do you see?
I see _____ triangles.	I see _____ squares.

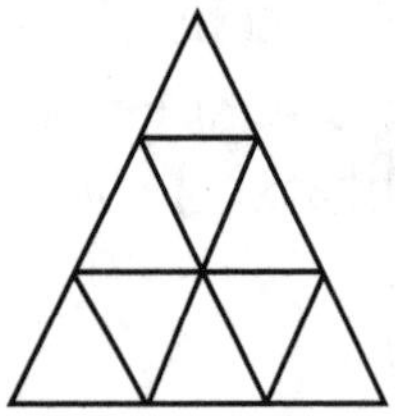

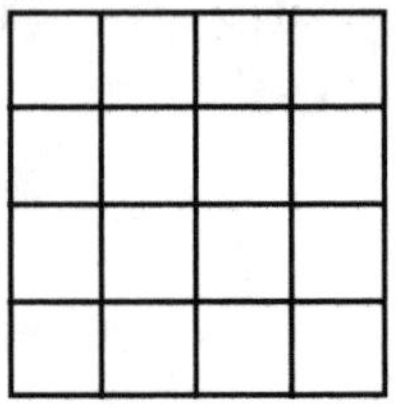

Sentence-a-Day

people   likes   to   picnic   there

_____

- -

_____

Circle the correct word that goes with each picture.

trees   threes

pine   picnic

cook   cool

mess   nest

fits   fish

lean   lion

Five-a-Day: Geometry, Patterns, and Shapes

Count the corners.	Count the corners.	Count the corners.
_____ corners	_____ corners	_____ corners

Make a shape that has exactly 6 corners.	Make a shape that does not have any corners.

Sentence-a-Day

a   square   have   four   sides

Find each hidden word. Color in each word.

C	I	R	C	L	E	U	D	O	W
D	I	A	M	O	N	D	X	P	S
B	R	Z	R	H	O	M	B	U	S
H	E	X	A	G	O	N	I	O	H
E	C	T	R	I	A	N	G	L	E
C	O	R	N	E	R	S	W	W	T
E	I	S	H	A	P	E	S	C	B
Q	R	E	C	T	A	N	G	L	E
V	S	Q	U	A	R	E	O	L	K
S	I	D	E	S	O	V	A	L	H

1. circle
2. corners
3. diamond
4. hexagon
5. oval
6. rectangle
7. rhombus
8. shapes
9. sides
10. square
11. triangle

Five-a-Day: Geometry, Patterns, and Shapes

Do the parts match? 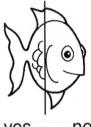 yes no	Do the parts match? 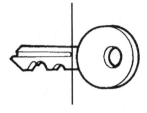 yes no	Do the parts match? 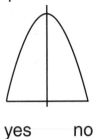 yes no
Make a square. Divide it into 2 equal parts.	Make a circle. Divide it into 2 equal parts.	

Sentence-a-Day

a   ball   are   a   sphere

_____

- -

_____

April						
Sunday	Monday	Tuesday	Wednesday	Thursday	Friday	Saturday
		1	2	3	4	5
6	7	8	9	10	11	12
13	14	15	16	17	18	19
20	21	22	23	24	25	26
27	28	29	30			

1. What is the name of this month?
   _____

2. How many days are in this month?
   _____

3. On what day of the week does April begin? _____

4. On what day of the week does April end ? _____

5. If I go to the zoo every Saturday, how many times will I be able to go this month?
   _____

Five-a-Day: Geometry, Patterns, and Shapes

Draw a line to make 2 equal parts.	Draw a line to make 2 equal parts.	Draw a line to make 2 equal parts. 

Make your own shape using only a square, a triangle, and a circle.	Make your own shape using only a rectangle, a diamond, and a square.

Sentence-a-Day

a   box   are   called   a   cube

_____

- -

_____

The verb in each sentence tells what is happening. When the action is occurring right now, add the *-ing* ending to the verb. When the action occurred in the past, add the *-ed* ending to the verb. For each sentence, circle the correct form of the verb.

1. Yesterday, we _walked_ _walking_ to the store.

2. Today, we are _walked_ _walking_ to school.

3. Johnny _laughed_ _laughing_ hard yesterday.

4. Today, Ramona is _laughed_ _laughing_ really hard.

Five-a-Day: Geometry, Patterns, and Shapes

Finish the pattern. A,A,S,A,A,S,A,A,S, ___, ___, ___, ___	Finish the pattern. R,R,U,R,R,U,R, ___, ___, ___, ___, ___	Finish the pattern. m,n,o,m,n,o, ___, ___, ___, ___, ___, ___
Make a pattern using only squares and circles.		Make a pattern using only triangles and rectangles.

Sentence-a-Day

mrs.   nelson   have   patterns   on   she   dress

_____

- -

_____

Add the correct ending (-ed or -ing) to the verb in each sentence.

1. At school, Jeremiah learn_____ to add numbers together.

2. Jessica is paint_____ a picture of a rainbow.

3. She watch_____ a lot of TV last night.

4. Lester is pick_____ out a book from the classroom library.

5. The flowers are really grow_____ in this nice weather.

6. Marcie clean_____ all of the tabletops and chairs.

Five-a-Day: Geometry, Patterns, and Shapes

Finish the pattern.	Finish the pattern.	Finish the pattern.
S,T,U,S,T,U,S, ___, ___, ___, ___, ___	X,Y,Z,X,Y, ___, ___, ___, ___, ___, ___	3,5,7,3,5,7,3, ___, ___, ___, ___, ___

Make a pattern using 3 different numbers.	Make a pattern using 3 different letters.

Sentence-a-Day

me   can   see   the   stars   and   stripes   pattern

_____

- -

_____

Add the correct ending (*-ed* or *-ing*) to the verb in each sentence.

1. Pablo is clean_____ his bedroom.

2. Henry scrubb_____ all of the pots and pans.

3. Mrs. Smith is driv_____ her car.

4. Ralph bark_____ all night at the cat.

5. Shirley pack_____ her suitcase.

Five-a-Day: Geometry, Patterns, and Shapes

Count the corners.	Count the corners.	Count the corners.
△	◯	⬠
_____ corners	_____ corners	_____ corners

Circle the shape that has 6 corners.	Circle the shape that has 3 corners.
☐ ⬡	△ ◯

Sentence-a-Day

lets   count   all   the   stars

_____

- -

_____

Add the correct ending (-ed or -ing) to the verb in each sentence.

1. The custodian is wash_____ all of the classroom windows.

2. Brent cook_____ spaghetti for dinner last night.

3. Holly collect_____ dolls when she was younger.

4. Timothy is play_____ with his toys.

5. Who is watch_____ the children?

6. I am call_____ my friend in Texas.

Five-a-Day: Geometry, Patterns, and Shapes

How many square units?	How many square units?	How many square units?
_____ square units.	_____ square units.	_____ square units.

Make a shape with 6 squares.	Make a shape with 9 squares.

Sentence-a-Day

we   is   gonna   make   box   kites

Add the correct ending (-ed or -ing) to the verb in each sentence.

1. Mary is typ_____ on the computer.

2. Is Garth rak_____ the leaves?

3. Sylvester chang_____ the channel.

4. George play_____ soccer with Larry last night.

5. Floyd repair_____ the van.

6. Mary Lou is wax_____ the truck.

Five-a-Day: Geometry, Patterns, and Shapes

Circle the shape that shows equal parts.	Circle the shape that shows equal parts.	Circle the shape that shows equal parts.

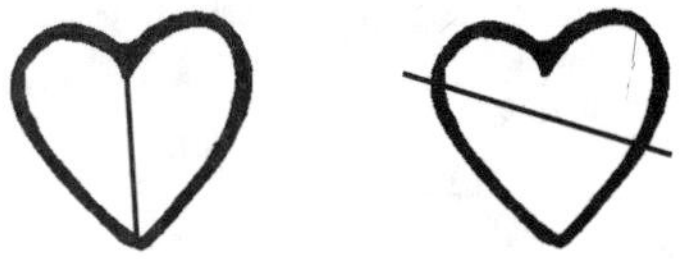

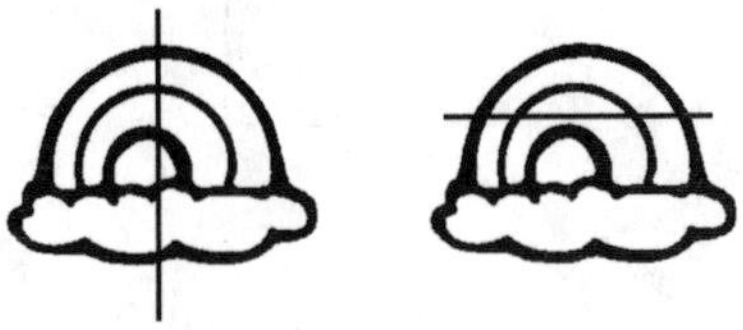

Circle the shape that shows 3 equal parts.	Circle the shape that shows 4 equal parts.
 	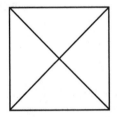 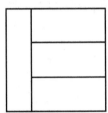

Sentence-a-Day

please   count   all   of   the   triangles

_____

- -

_____

Read the scrambled sentence. Write the words in the correct order.

a   lot   There   of   different   are   shapes.

_____

- -

_____

Five-a-Day: Add and Subtract to 18

Add.	Subtract.	Add.
8 + 9 ___	13 − 6 ___	7 + 4 ___

Jamal had 5 rolling pins. If 3 of them rolled off of the table, how many are left on the table? There are _____ rolling pins left.	Alvin found 16 cardboard boxes. He flattened 8 of them. How many of them had not been flattened? _____ boxes had not been flattened.

Sentence-a-Day

lets   play   the   shapes   game

Read the scrambled words. Write the sentence correctly on the lines.

cooking is The hamburgers. man

_____

Five-a-Day: Geometry, Patterns, and Shapes

Color in the shape to show ½.	Color in the shape to show ½.	Color in the shape to show ½.

 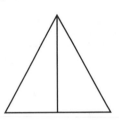 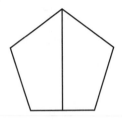

Circle the shape that shows ½.	Circle the shape that shows ½.

 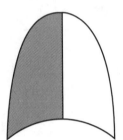 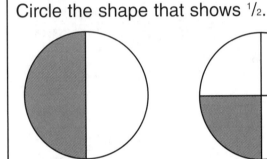 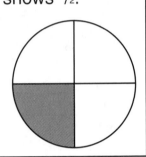

Sentence-a-Day

mr   menio   cutted   the   cake   in   half

Rhyming words have the same ending sounds.

For example, cat and hat are two words that rhyme.

Draw a line to match each of the two pictures that rhyme.

Name _____

Five-a-Day: Geometry, Patterns, and Shapes

Color in the shape to show ⅓.	Color in the shape to show ⅓.	Color in the shape to show ⅓.
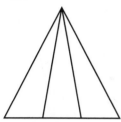	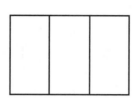	

Circle the shape that shows ⅓.	Circle the shape that shows ⅓.
 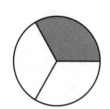	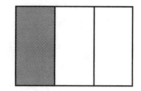 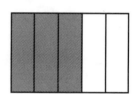

Sentence-a-Day

what   fruit   come   in   three's

_____

- -

_____

Rhyming words have the same ending sounds.

For example, cat and hat are two words that rhyme.

Draw a line to match each of the two pictures that rhyme.

Five-a-Day: Geometry, Patterns, and Shapes

Color in the shape to show ¼.	Color in the shape to show ¼.	Color in the shape to show ¼.
	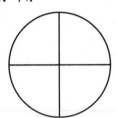	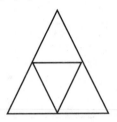

Circle the shape that shows ¼.	Circle the shape that shows ¼.
 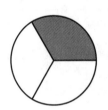	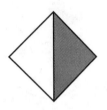 

Sentence-a-Day

we   ates   a   fourth   of   the   pie

_____

- -

_____

Rhyming words have the same ending sounds.

For example, cat and hat are two words that rhyme.

Draw a line to match each of the two pictures that rhyme.

Five-a-Day: Geometry, Patterns, and Shapes

Color in the shape to show ¹/₅.	Color in the shape to show ¹/₅.	Color in the shape to show ¹/₅.
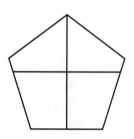	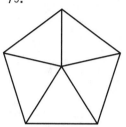	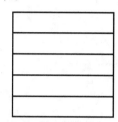

Circle the shape that shows ¹/₅.	Circle the shape that shows ¹/₅.
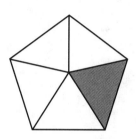 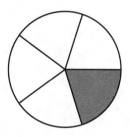	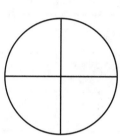

Sentence-a-Day

one   finger   are   a   fifth   of   my   hand

- -

Rhyming words have the same ending sounds.

For example, cat and hat are two words that rhyme.

Draw a line to match each of the two words that rhyme.

rug	**three**
boat	**tag**
bee	**kite**
flag	**coat**
sad	**mad**
bite	**book**
look	**bug**

Five-a-Day: Geometry, Patterns, and Shapes

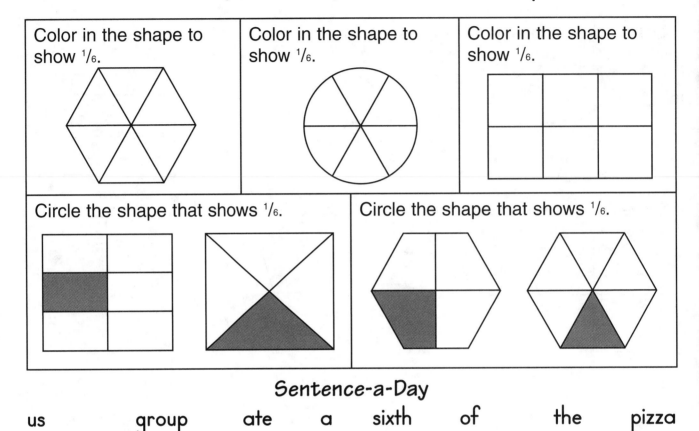

Color in the shape to show ¹/₆.

Color in the shape to show ¹/₆.

Color in the shape to show ¹/₆.

Circle the shape that shows ¹/₆.

Circle the shape that shows ¹/₆.

Sentence-a-Day

us   group   ate   a   sixth   of   the   pizza

Rhyming words have the same ending sounds.

For example, cat and hat are two words that rhyme.

Draw a line to match each of the two words that rhyme.

muffin	might
near	hear
jig	puffin
lot	hot
night	pig
yarn	cow
how	barn

Name _____

Five-a-Day: Geometry, Patterns, and Shapes

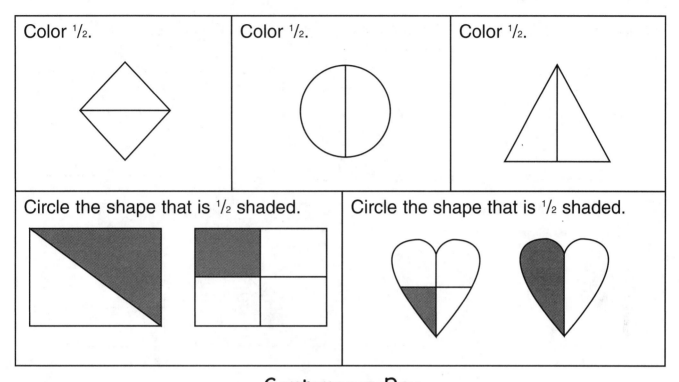

Color ½.

Color ½.

Color ½.

Circle the shape that is ½ shaded.

Circle the shape that is ½ shaded.

Sentence-a-Day

us   class   like   learning   about   fractions

_____

- -

_____

Rhyming words have the same ending sounds.

For example, cat and hat are two words that rhyme.

Draw a line to match each of the two words that rhyme.

rough	**boy**
hen	**ape**
reed	**solar**
tape	**home**
polar	**tough**
gnome	**pen**
soy	**seed**

Five-a-Day: Geometry, Patterns, and Shapes

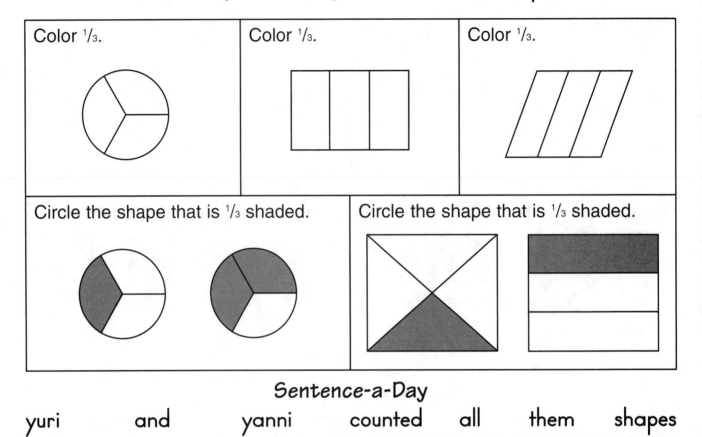

Color ⅓.	Color ⅓.	Color ⅓.
Circle the shape that is ⅓ shaded.		Circle the shape that is ⅓ shaded.

Sentence-a-Day

yuri   and   yanni   counted   all   them   shapes

Adding *'s* to a word shows ownership. In each sentence below, add an *'s* to each word to show ownership.

1. That is Jason_____ red scarf.

2. Sylvia_____ gold shoes are too small.

3. The dog_____ blanket needs to be washed.

4. Dad_____ bicycle is a 10 speed.

5. Mom_____ computer has a lot of software on it.

Five-a-Day: Geometry, Patterns, and Shapes

Color ¼.	Color ¼.	Color ¼.

Circle the shape that is ¼ shaded.

Circle the shape that is ¼ shaded.

Sentence-a-Day

harry   cutted   it   into   four   parts

Adding *'s* to a word shows ownership. In each sentence below add an *'s* to each word to show ownership.

1. The snail_____ shell was left behind in our garden.

2. Penelope_____ reading book was in her desk.

3. The bear_____ name is Teddy.

4. The bird_____ cage is in the kitchen.

5. Justin_____ birthday party was a surprise.

Five-a-Day: Geometry, Patterns, and Shapes

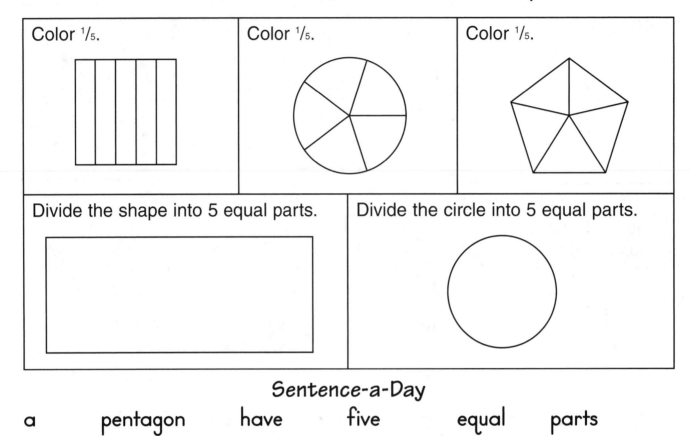

| Color ⅕. | Color ⅕. | Color ⅕. |

| Divide the shape into 5 equal parts. | Divide the circle into 5 equal parts. |

Sentence-a-Day

a   pentagon   have   five   equal   parts

_____

- -

_____

A digraph is two letters that work together to make one sound. Use the digraphs in the word bank to help you write the beginning digraph for each word.

ch   ch   ch   th   th   th

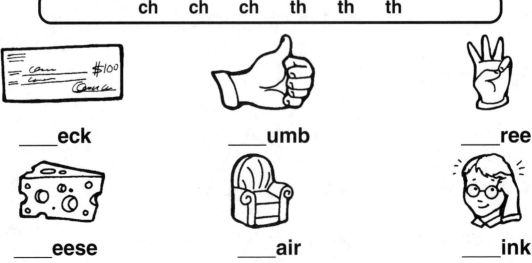

____eck   ____umb   ____ree

____eese   ____air   ____ink

Five-a-Day: Add and Subtract to 18

Add.	Subtract.	Add.
9 + 9 ___	16 − 3 ___	9 + 8 ___

Circle the correct answer. King Joseph had 9 kingdoms. He sold all of them. How many kingdoms does he have left? 18 kingdoms 0 kingdoms	Circle the correct answer. Mrs. Jones had 9 workers in her store. She hired 7 more. How many workers does she now have? 2 workers 16 workers

Sentence-a-Day

bud   and   lou   seen   a   movie

- -

A digraph is two letters that work together to make one sound. Use the digraphs in the word bank to help you write the beginning digraph for each word.

sh   sh   sh   wh   wh   wh

____ark   ____eel   ____ale

____eep   ____arpener   ____eelbarow

Five-a-Day: Geometry, Patterns, and Shapes

What part is shaded?	What part is shaded?	What part is shaded?
$\frac{1}{2}$ $\frac{1}{3}$ $\frac{1}{4}$	$\frac{1}{2}$ $\frac{1}{3}$ $\frac{1}{4}$	$\frac{1}{2}$ $\frac{1}{3}$ $\frac{1}{4}$

I had a whole pie. I cut it in $\frac{1}{2}$. How many pieces of pie do I have now? I have _____ pieces of pie.	Rocky ordered a pizza. The pizza was cut into 4 equal pieces. Rocky ate half of the pizza. How many pieces did Rocky eat? Rocky ate _____ pieces of pizza.

Sentence-a-Day

betty   lou   ate   one-half   of   the   dessert

_____

- -

A digraph is two letters that work together to make one sound. Use the digraphs in the word bank to help you write the beginning digraph for each word.

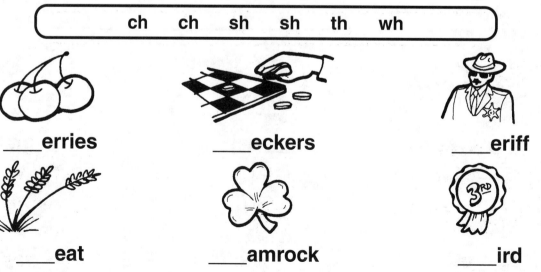

| ch   ch   sh   sh   th   wh |

____erries   ____eckers   ____eriff

____eat   ____amrock   ____ird

Five-a-Day: Geometry, Patterns, and Shapes

What part is shaded?	What part is shaded?	What part is shaded?
$\frac{1}{3}$ $\frac{1}{4}$ $\frac{1}{5}$	$\frac{1}{3}$ $\frac{1}{4}$ $\frac{1}{5}$	$\frac{1}{3}$ $\frac{1}{4}$ $\frac{1}{5}$

Ricky had 9 marbles. He kept $\frac{1}{3}$. He gave $\frac{1}{3}$ to Sonya and $\frac{1}{3}$ to Len. How many marbles does each person now have? Each person has _____ marbles.	Marilyn had 5 houses. She sold $\frac{1}{5}$ of them. How many houses did she keep? Marilyn kept _____ houses.

Sentence-a-Day

this   are   the   fifth   time   we   saw   the   movie

_____

- -

A digraph is two letters that work together to make one sound. Use the digraphs in the word bank to help you write the beginning digraph for each word.

ch   ch   sh   sh   th   wh

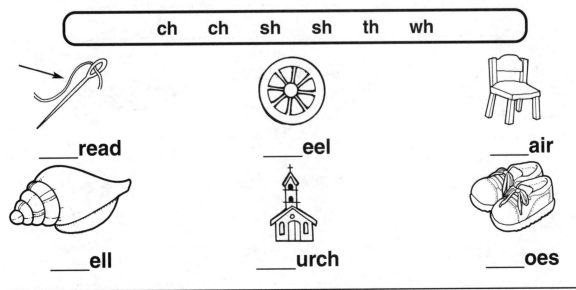

____read

____eel

____air

____ell

____urch

____oes

Five-a-Day: Geometry, Patterns, and Shapes

What part is shaded?	What part is shaded?	What part is shaded?
		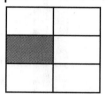
$\frac{1}{4}$ $\frac{1}{5}$ $\frac{1}{2}$	$\frac{1}{2}$ $\frac{1}{3}$ $\frac{1}{4}$	$\frac{1}{2}$ $\frac{1}{6}$ $\frac{1}{4}$

Make a pizza. Cut it into 6 equal pieces. How many cuts did you make? I made _____ straight cuts.	Draw a cookie. Cut it into 4 equal parts. Color $\frac{3}{4}$ of the cookie.

Sentence-a-Day

us   want   to   see   it   for   the   sixth   time

_____

- -

_____

To make nouns that end in *y* plural (more than one), drop the *y* and add *ies* to the end of the noun. Look at each picture and draw a line to match it to either the singular name or the plural name.

strawberry

pony

strawberries

ponies

Five-a-Day: Geometry, Patterns, and Shapes

What part is shaded?	What part is shaded?	What part is shaded?
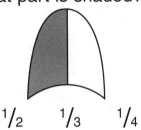 $\frac{1}{2}$ $\frac{1}{3}$ $\frac{1}{4}$	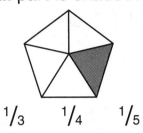 $\frac{1}{3}$ $\frac{1}{4}$ $\frac{1}{5}$	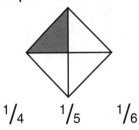 $\frac{1}{4}$ $\frac{1}{5}$ $\frac{1}{6}$

How many squares of equal size can you make out of the square below?	How many triangles of equal size can you make out of the triangle below?
I made _____ squares of equal size.	I made _____ triangles of equal size.

Sentence-a-Day

jessica   use   fractions   all   of   the   time

_____

- -

_____

To make nouns that end in *y* plural (more than one), drop the *y* and add *ies* to the end of the noun. Look at each picture and draw a line to match it to either the singular noun or the plural noun.

candy

puppy

candies

puppies

Five-a-Day: Geometry, Patterns, and Shapes

Draw a square. Color ¼ of the square.	Draw a triangle. Color ½ of the triangle.	Draw a circle. Color ⅓ of the circle.
Draw a rectangle. Color ³⁄₆ of the rectangle.		Draw a hexagon. Color ¼ of the hexagon.

Sentence-a-Day

did   you   learn   anything   new   today

To make nouns that end in *y* plural (more than one), drop the *y* and add *ies* to the end of the noun. Look at each picture and draw a line to match it to either the singular noun or the plural noun.

fairy

butterfly

fairies

butterflies

Five-a-Day: Time

Circle the correct time.	Circle the correct time.	Circle the correct time.

5:30 6:30	1:30 7:30	8:00 8:30

Make the clock show ½ hour later.	Make the clock show ½ hour later.

5:30 ___ : ___ ___	2:00 ___ : ___ ___

Sentence-a-Day

we   goes   to   lunch   at   11:30

_____

- -

_____

To make nouns that end in *y* plural (more than one), drop the *y* and add *ies* to the end of the noun. Look at each picture and draw a line to match it to either the singular noun or the plural noun.

baby

lady

babies

ladies

Five-a-Day: Time

Write the time.	Write the time.	Write the time.

___ : ___ ___	___ : ___ ___	___ : ___ ___

Make the clock show 1 hour later.		Make the clock show 1 hour earlier.	
11:00	___ : ___ ___	1:00	___ : ___ ___

Sentence-a-Day

ms   duncan   teached   computers   at   3:00

_____

- -

_____

To make nouns that end in *y* plural (more than one), drop the *y* and add *ies* to the end of the noun. Look at each picture and draw a line to match it to either the singular noun or the plural noun.

daddy

body

daddies

bodies

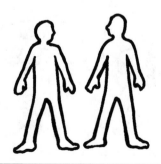

Five-a-Day: Time

Circle the correct time.	Circle the correct time.	Circle the correct time.

2:30 9:30	1:00 11:00	4:30 6:00

Use A.M. or P.M. to show the correct time of day.	Use A.M. or P.M. to show the correct time of day.
Laura goes to bed at 8:00 _____ each night.	Peter eats lunch at 11:30 _____ each morning.

Sentence-a-Day

can   you   meet   us   at   2:00 P.M.

_____

- -

_____

To make nouns that end in *y* plural (more than one), drop the *y* and add *ies* to the end of the noun. Look at each picture and draw a line to match it to either the singular noun or the plural noun.

fly

story

flies

stories

Five-a-Day: Time

Write the time.	Write the time.	Write the time.

____ : ____ ____	____ : ____ ____	____ : ____ ____

Use A.M. or P.M. to show the correct time of day.	Use A.M. or P.M. to show the correct time of day.
Ozzie Owl wakes up at 3:00 _____ each morning.	Henrietta Hippo takes her bath each night at 7:00 _____ .

Sentence-a-Day

i   calls   you   last   night   at   10:00 P.M.

_____

- -

To make nouns that end in *y* plural (more than one), drop the *y* and add *ies* to the end of the noun. Look at each picture and draw a line to match it to either the singular noun or the plural noun.

cherry

berry

cherries

berries

Five-a-Day: Add and Subtract 2-Digit Numbers

Add.	Subtract.	Subtract.
$\begin{array}{r} 47 \\ + 21 \\ \hline \end{array}$	$\begin{array}{r} 60 \\ - 20 \\ \hline \end{array}$	$\begin{array}{r} 49 \\ - 36 \\ \hline \end{array}$

How would you solve the problem? Circle add or subtract.

Polly had 49 flowers. If 36 of them died, how many are left?

add   subtract

How would you solve the problem? Circle add or subtract.

William had 71 red spots on one arm and 28 red spots on the other arm. How many spots did he have in all?

add   subtract

Sentence-a-Day

is   them   red   spots   called   chicken   pox

_____

- -

S	P	U	P	P	I	E	S	T	B	D	P
T	J	W	L	F	L	W	F	G	A	A	O
O	Z	B	A	C	A	N	L	C	B	D	G
R	X	G	D	D	D	D	Y	C	I	D	B
I	B	I	I	X	Y	K	L	Y	E	I	V
E	B	V	E	S	K	G	A	N	S	E	Y
S	K	G	S	D	A	D	D	Y	P	S	G
R	Y	L	S	X	P	A	Y	P	U	O	D
F	J	A	T	K	U	C	R	W	B	V	R
R	U	N	O	R	P	D	R	S	U	A	W
Q	S	C	R	O	P	Y	B	B	A	B	Y
H	D	Z	Y	Q	Y	H	X	J	S	F	E

Find each hidden word, across or down. Color the word in.

1. baby
2. babies
3. daddy
4. daddies
5. lady
6. ladies
7. puppy
8. puppies
9. story
10. stories

Five-a-Day: Add and Subtract to 12

Subtract.	Subtract.	Subtract.
12 – 6 = _____	11 – 6 = _____	8 – 4 = _____
9 – 2 = _____	10 – 6 = _____	6 – 5 = _____

How would you solve this problem? Circle add or subtract.	How would you solve this problem? Circle add or subtract.
Kim picked 7 flowers. If 6 wilted on the way home, how many are left?	Tracy had 8 letters. She mailed five of them. How many are left?
add subtract	add subtract

Sentence-a-Day

pablo   he   had   chicken   pox,   too

_____

- -

_____

To make nouns that end in *y* plural (more than one), drop the *y* and add *ies* to the end of the noun. Look at each picture and circle either the singular form of the noun or the plural form of the noun.

fry fries   **fly flies**   **berry berries**   **pony ponies**

Five-a-Day: Add and Subtract to 12

Subtract. $$\begin{array}{r} 11 \\ -\ 6 \\ \hline \end{array}$$	Subtract. $$\begin{array}{r} 9 \\ -\ 5 \\ \hline \end{array}$$	Subtract. $$\begin{array}{r} 10 \\ -\ 4 \\ \hline \end{array}$$

How would you solve this problem? Circle add or subtract.	How would you solve this problem? Circle add or subtract.
Cybill had 5 phone calls, but only 2 messages. How many did not leave a message?	Jesse bought 9 stamps but 3 were stuck together. How many stamps was Jesse able to use?
add subtract	add subtract

Sentence-a-Day

the   new   stamp   it   has   bears   on   it

To make nouns that end in *y* plural (more than one), drop the *y* and add *ies* to the end of the noun. Look at each picture and circle either the singular form of the noun or the plural form of the noun.

fairy fairies   **daddy daddies**   **lady ladies**   **baby babies**

Five-a-Day: Add and Subtract to 12

Solve.	Solve.	Solve.
$6 + 4 =$ _____	$7 + 2 =$ _____	$5 + 3 =$ _____
$10 - 6 =$ _____	$9 - 7 =$ _____	$8 - 5 =$ _____

Use 3, 9, and 12 to make two addition problems.	Use 3, 9, and 12 to make two subtraction problems.
_____ + _____ = _____	_____ − _____ = _____
_____ + _____ = _____	_____ − _____ = _____

Sentence-a-Day

mr   early   buyed   a   whole   set

_____

- -

_____

To make nouns that end in *y* plural (more than one), drop the *y* and add *ies* to the end of the noun. Look at each picture and circle either the singular form of the noun or the plural form of the noun.

puppy   puppies   candy   candies   penny   pennies   story   stories

Five-a-Day: Add and Subtract to 12

Solve.	Solve.	Solve.
6 + 1 = _____	9 + 3 = _____	4 + 8 = _____
7 – 6 = _____	12 – 3 = _____	12 – 8 = _____

Use 4, 8, and 12 to make two addition problems.	Use 6, 4, and 10 to make two subtraction problems.
_____ + _____ = _____ _____ + _____ = _____	_____ – _____ = _____ _____ – _____ = _____

Sentence-a-Day

ain't   he   collecting   teddy   bears

_____

- -

_____

I	B	G	U	J	W	D	S	F	Q	X	E
N	U	X	U	Z	F	X	U	L	Y	W	X
Q	T	E	Q	G	G	T	U	Y	E	S	M
C	T	U	W	D	H	O	M	T	E	S	Z
A	E	B	B	U	T	T	E	R	F	L	Y
Q	R	O	B	R	B	F	E	B	H	R	V
O	F	D	E	J	E	A	U	G	Q	G	F
Z	L	I	R	B	R	I	H	A	T	D	B
A	I	E	R	O	R	R	J	Q	I	K	K
C	E	S	I	D	Y	Y	O	S	I	R	W
N	S	O	E	Y	F	L	I	E	S	B	M
G	L	W	S	F	A	I	R	I	E	S	M

Find each hidden word, across or down. Color the word in.

1. berry
2. berries
3. body
4. bodies
5. butterfly
6. butterflies
7. fairy
8. fairies
9. fly
10. flies

Five-a-Day: Add and Subtract to 12

Solve.

5 + 8 = _____

13 − 8 = _____

Solve.

9 + 3 = _____

12 − 9 = _____

Solve.

7 + 5 = _____

12 − 5 = _____

Use 1, 11, and 12 to make two addition problems.

_____ + _____ = _____

_____ + _____ = _____

Use 1, 11, and 12 to make two subtraction problems.

_____ − _____ = _____

_____ − _____ = _____

Sentence-a-Day

he   have   a   big   bear   collection

_____

_____

Complete each sentence with the correct word from the word bank.

baby   fairy   strawberry   puppies   pennies   candies

The tooth _____ visited Tansy and left her some

_____ . With her money, Tansy bought three chocolate

_____ and a _____ doll. Tansy did not give her two _____

any of the candy. Instead, she fed them one _____ .

Five-a-Day: Place Value

Write the number.	Write the number.	Write the number.
4 tens 7 ones	8 tens 9 ones	1 ten 3 ones
_____	_____	_____

Use > or <.	Use > or <.
3 tens ◯ 8 tens	9 ones ◯ 5 ones

Sentence-a-Day

sharon   seen   nine   big   lions

_____

- -

_____

Complete each sentence with the correct word from the word bank.

> **cherries   body   ladies   puppy   pony   cherry**

The white _____ woke up. His _____ was covered

by a blanket. He started barking and scared five _____ who

were eating ripe _____ . The ladies hopped onto a _____

and rode away. The puppy ate the last _____ .

Five-a-Day: Place Value

Write the number that is 1 more.	Write the number that is 1 more.	Write the number that is 1 more.
37, _____	32, _____	14, _____
59, _____	45, _____	83, _____

Use > or <.

1 ten 1 one ◯ 1 ten

Use > or <.

3 ones ◯ 1 ten

Sentence-a-Day

the   lion   it   was   roaring

_____

- -

_____

F	Z	R	D	W	V	P	P	E	P	E	V
R	C	A	N	D	Y	E	M	E	O	N	T
Y	P	K	H	O	R	N	T	S	N	M	D
J	O	F	V	A	N	N	R	L	Y	C	Y
X	N	R	O	I	M	Y	J	W	C	I	L
H	I	I	Z	H	T	O	F	T	H	V	K
N	E	E	X	A	Z	O	B	N	E	F	V
Q	S	S	C	H	E	R	R	Y	R	R	F
P	E	N	N	I	E	S	V	D	R	C	T
I	C	A	N	D	I	E	S	Y	I	H	I
D	T	V	S	P	T	G	D	A	E	B	U
W	F	D	O	A	C	L	T	R	S	O	B

Find each hidden word, across or down. Color the word in.

1. candy
2. candies
3. cherry
4. cherries
5. fry
6. fries
7. penny
8. pennies
9. pony
10. ponies

Name ____________________ Practice 183

Five-a-Day: Place Value

Write the number that is 1 less.	Write the number that is 1 less.	Write the number that is 1 less.
______ , 65	______ , 40	______ , 62
______ ,100	______ , 91	______ , 60

Use > or <.	Use > or <.
3 tens 1 one ◯ 5 tens	2 tens 4 ones ◯ 1 ten 8 ones

Sentence-a-Day

does you see sharon running away

____

A long vowel says its letter's name. Write the missing long vowel in each word. (Vowels are a, e, i, o, and u.)

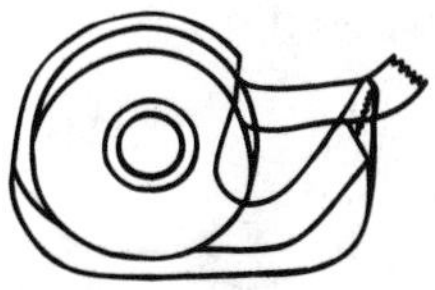

t ____ pe

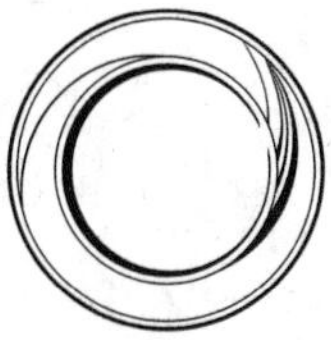

pl ____ te

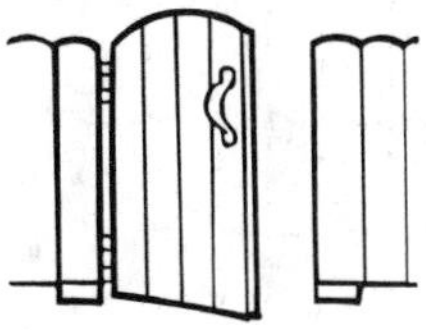

g ____ te

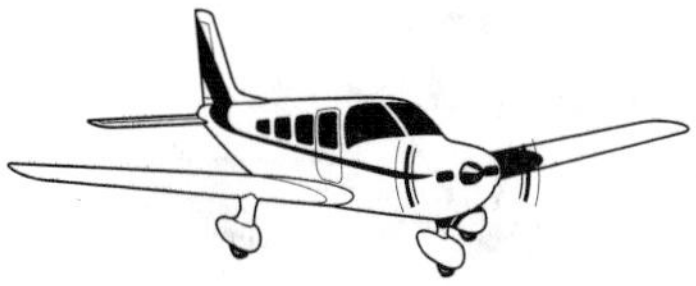

pl ____ ne

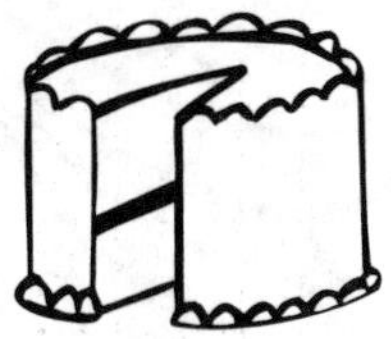

c ____ ke

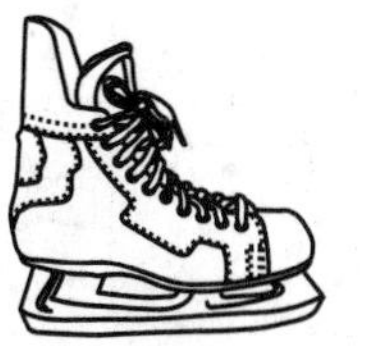

sk ____ te

Five-a-Day: Place Value

Write the number that comes in between.	Write the number that comes in between.	Write the number that comes in between.
46, _____ , 48	59, _____ , 61	60, _____ , 62
98, _____ , 100	83, _____ , 85	17, _____ , 19

Use > or <.

9 tens ◯ 10 tens

Use. > or <.

3 tens 6 ones ◯ 6 tens 3 ones

Sentence-a-Day

me   likes   the   zebras   best

_____

- -

_____

A long vowel says its letter's name. Write the missing long vowel in each word. (Vowels are a, e, i, o, and u.)

h ____ ar

dr ____ am

s ____ al

s ____ at

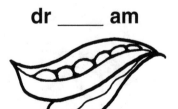

p ____ as

l ____ af

Five-a-Day: Place Value

Write even or odd.	Write even or odd.	Write even or odd.
22, 24, 26, 28	41, 43, 45, 47	65, 67, 69, 71
_____	_____	_____

Mystery Number: I am an even number. I am greater than 30 and less than 50. When you count by 10's you say my name. What number am I?	Mystery Number: I am an odd number. I am greater than 80 and less than 90. When you count by 5's you say my name. What number am I?
The mystery number is _____ .	The mystery number is _____ .

Sentence-a-Day

which   animal   does   karen   like   best

_____

- -

_____

A long vowel says its letter's name. Write the missing long vowel in each word. (Vowels are a, e, i, o, and u.)

pr ____ ze

m ____ ce

b ____ ke

h ____ ve

r ____ ce

l ____ me

Five-a-Day: Comparing Numbers

Circle the greater number.	Circle the greater number.	Circle the greater number.
20 97	6 7	24 41

Issac has 22 peanuts. Pam has 17 more peanuts than Issac. How many peanuts does Pam have?	Patty has 12 headbands. Cathy has 2 fewer headbands than Patty. How many headbands does Cathy have?
Pam has _____ peanuts.	Cathy has _____ headbands.

Sentence-a-Day

me   thinks   she   likes   the   giraffes   best

_____

- -

_____

A long vowel says its letter's name. Write the missing long vowel in each word. (Vowels are a, e, i, o, and u.)

r ___ w

sm ___ ke

b ___ at

g ___ at

br ___ ke

w ___ ke

Five-a-Day: Comparing Numbers

Circle the greater number.	Circle the greater number.	Circle the greater number.
32 74	51 80	97 95

Candace went on the camel ride 41 times. Patrice went on the camel ride 18 times. How many times did the girls ride the camel in all? The girls rode the camel _____ times.	Sean fed the monkey 31 peanuts. Thomas fed the monkey 14 peanuts. How many peanuts did the monkey eat? The monkey ate _____ peanuts.

Sentence-a-Day

us   class   went   to   the   chaffee   zoo

_____

- -

_____

A long vowel says its letter's name. Write the missing long vowel in each word. (Vowels are a, e, i, o, and u.)

____ nicorn   pl ____ me   m ____ le

fl ____ te   c ____ be   fr ____ it

Five-a-Day: Comparing Numbers

Circle the smaller number.	Circle the smaller number.	Circle the smaller number.
29 32	4 3	98 86

Zipporah saw 15 paw prints. Lacey saw 3 fewer paw prints than Zipporah. How many paw prints did Lacey see?	Misty saw 43 turtles. Mabel saw 10 fewer turtles than Misty. How many turtles did Mabel see?
Lacey saw _____ paw prints.	Mabel saw _____ turtles.

Sentence-a-Day

mr   houston   took   us   on   friday

_____

- -

_____

A long vowel says its letter's name. Write the missing long vowel in each word. (Vowels are a, e, i, o, and u.)

ph ____ ne   p ____ e   br ____ de

g ____ te   ____ be   r ____ pe

Five-a-Day: Comparing Numbers

Circle the smaller number.	Circle the smaller number.	Circle the smaller number.
17 71	74 64	32 35

There were 71 birds in the bird show. Angelica saw only 40 of the birds. How many birds did Angelica not see?	The zookeeper had 86 crickets in a jar. She gave the tortoise 43 of the crickets. How many crickets does the zookeeper have left?
Angelica did not see _____ birds.	The zookeeper has _____ crickets.

Sentence-a-Day

do   an   elephant   weigh   a   ton

_____

- -

_____

A long vowel says its letter's name. Write the missing long vowel in each word. (Vowels are a, e, i, o, and u.)

h ____ se   d ____ me   st ____ am

m ____ il   t ____ be   c ____ ke

Five-a-Day: Comparing Numbers

Use > or <.	Use > or <.	Use > or <.
18 ◯ 15	52 ◯ 37	41 ◯ 25

8 + 1 ◯ 6

_____ is greater than _____ .

6 + 6 ◯ 9

_____ is greater than _____ .

Sentence-a-Day

an   elephant   weighs   more   than   a   car

A long vowel says its letter's name. Write the missing long vowel in each word. (Vowels are a, e, i, o, and u.)

v ____ ne

gr ____ pes

fr ____ es

b ____ te

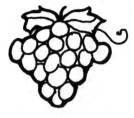

fr ____ it

b ____ ne

Five-a-Day: Place Value

Write the number of cubes. 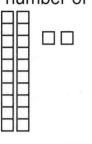 _____	Write the number of cubes. 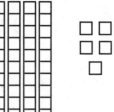 _____	Write the number of cubes. _____

Circle the correct answer.	Circle the correct answer.
$9 - 3 =$ _____	$9, 10,$ _____
5 10 12 Not Here	9 10 11 Not Here

Sentence-a-Day

why   do   a   monkey   have   a   tail

_____

- -

A long vowel says its letter's name. Write the missing long vowel in each word. (Vowels are a, e, i, o, and u.)

s ____ al

sn ____ ke

b ____ ne

h ____ rse

m ____ ce

wh ____ le

Five-a-Day: Place Value

Write the number of cubes. 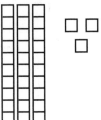 _____	Write the number of cubes. 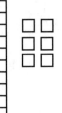 _____	Write the number of cubes. 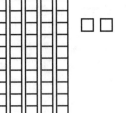 _____

Circle the correct answer. 6, 7, 8, _____ 9　　10　　11　　12	Circle the correct answer. $12 - 5 =$ _____ 6　　7　　8　　9

Sentence-a-Day

they　　　uses　　　them　　　for　　　balance

_____

- -

A long vowel says its letter's name. Write the missing long vowel in each word. (Vowels are a, e, i, o, and u.)

sn ____ il

j ____ ice

n ____ tes

cl ____ thes

ch ____ ld

dr ____ am

Five-a-Day: Place Value

Draw the number of tens and ones needed in cubes to make 21.	Draw the number of tens and ones needed in cubes to make 33.	Draw the number of tens and ones needed in cubes to make 18.

Circle the correct answer. 5 + 6 = ____ 6 11 12 Not here	Circle the correct answer. 10 + 2 = ____ 9 11 13 Not here

Sentence-a-Day

we're   gonna   watch   the   seal   swim

_____

- -

_____

Read the scrambled sentence. Write the words in the correct order.

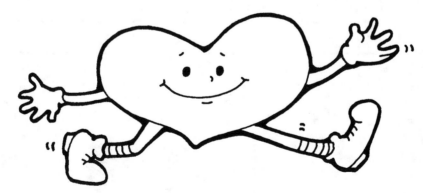

walking   you   the   Did   see   heart?

_____

- -

_____

Five-a-Day: Place Value

Draw the number of tens and ones needed in cubes to make 9.	Draw the number of tens and ones needed in cubes to make 25.	Draw the number of tens and ones needed in cubes to make 40.

Draw the hands to show the correct time. The camel rides begin at 10:00 A.M. 	Draw the hands to show the correct time. The bird show is over at 11:30 A.M. 

Sentence-a-Day

me   and   india   liked   the   rhino   the   best

_____

- -

_____

Write the correct blend at the end of each word.

| st | nd | nd | st |

ha ____   **ba** ____   **ne** ____   **fir** ____

Five-a-Day: Place Value

Draw the number of tens and ones needed in cubes to make 37.	Draw the number of tens and ones needed in cubes to make 12.	Draw the number of tens and ones needed in cubes to make 54.

Draw the hands to show the correct time. The zookeeper feeds the snakes at 2:00 P.M. 	Draw the hands to show the correct time. The bison goes for a walk at 5:00 P.M. 

Sentence-a-Day

can   us   go   to   the   zoo   again

_____

- -

_____

Write the correct blend at the end of each word.

nt   rm   rt   st

a ____   re ____   airpo ____   ala ____

Five-a-Day: Addition Facts to 18

Add.	Add.	Add.
7 + 4 = _____	9 + 5 = _____	7 + 9 = _____
4 + 9 = _____	8 + 7 = _____	7 + 6 = _____

Jenny made 8 kites. Tammy made 6 kites. How many kites did they make in all?

They made _____ kites in all.

Chester saw 6 clouds that looked like lions and 9 clouds that looked like tigers. How many clouds did Chester see in all?

Chester saw _____ clouds in all.

Sentence-a-Day

the   wind   are   blowing   hard   today

_____

- -

_____

Write the correct blend at the end of each word.

ng   nk   nt   rn

apartme _____   **ba** _____   **ba** _____   **ba** _____

Five-a-Day: Addition Facts to 18

Solve.	Solve.	Solve.
$6 +$ _____ $= 14$	_____ $+ 9 = 13$	$6 +$ _____ $= 15$
$8 +$ _____ $= 15$	_____ $+ 8 = 14$	$5 +$ _____ $= 13$

I have 13 books from my brother and sister. My sister gave me 7 of the books. How many did my brother give me? My brother gave me _____ books.	Dad has 12 kites. If 7 of them are box kites, how many are not box kites? _____ are not box kites.

Sentence-a-Day

its   too   windy   to   fly   a   kite

Write the correct blend at the end of each word.

lt   mp   rd   rd

be _____   **billboa** _____   **bli** _____   **bi** _____

Five-a-Day: Addition Facts to 18

Add.	Add.	Add.
9 + 9 = _____	8 + 8 = _____	7 + 9 = _____
4 + 8 = _____	9 + 3 = _____	13 + 0 = _____

There were 9 dandelions in Terri's front yard and 7 in her backyard. How many dandelions were there in all?	Doug collects flowers. He has 5 roses and 9 wildflowers in his collection. How many flowers does Doug have in all?
There were _____ dandelions in all.	Doug has _____ flowers in all.

Sentence-a-Day

plants   needs   soil,   water,   and   sunlight

_____

- -

_____

Write the correct blend at the end of each word.

| ld | mp | rd | st |

ca _____   ca _____   ca _____   so _____

Five-a-Day: Addition Facts to 18

Add.	Add.	Add.
3 + 3 + 4 = _____	2 + 2 + 6 = _____	6 + 2 + 4 = _____
6 + 3 + 3 = _____	4 + 4 + 4 = _____	3 + 3 + 6 = _____

Rosita had 5 yellow pencils, 1 pink pencil, and 2 green pencils. How many pencils did she have in all?	Luke had 4 baseball gloves, 5 bats, and 4 uniforms. How many pieces of baseball equipment did Luke have in all?
Rosita had _____ pencils in all.	Luke had _____ pieces in all.

Sentence-a-Day

are   a   cactus   prickly

_____

- -

_____

Write the correct blend at the end of each word.

| mp | rk | rn | st |

la _____   **li** _____   **la** _____   **lante** _____

Name _____

Five-a-Day: Addition Facts to 18

Add.	Add.	Add.
1 + 4 + 5 = ____	5 + 4 + 5 = ____	2 + 5 + 3 = ____
2 + 6 + 2 = ____	6 + 3 + 2 = ____	4 + 3 + 3 = ____

Penny has 2 red rings, 7 green rings, and 1 white ring. How many rings does Penny have in all?

Penny has _____ rings in all.

Christopher has 5 pennies, 2 nickels, and 7 dimes. How many coins does he have in all?

Christopher has _____ coins in all.

Sentence-a-Day

cactuses   grows   in   the   hot   desert

Write the correct blend at the end of each word.

| ng | rd | sk | st |

locu ____   **M. L. Ki** ____, **Jr.**   **ma** ____   **liza** ____

Five-a-Day: Subtraction Facts to 18

Subtract.	Subtract.	Subtract.
13 – 4 = _____	14 – 6 = _____	15 – 8 = _____
15 – 7 = _____	13 – 5 = _____	14 – 9 = _____

Trevor saw 13 cactuses. If 8 of them had flowers, how many cactuses did not have flowers?	Dennis earned 14 game points. He needs 18 points to win. How many more points must he earn to win?
_____cactuses did not have flowers.	He must earn _____ more points.

Sentence-a-Day

bees   makes   honey   from   nectar

_____

- -

Write the correct blend at the end of each word.

| nt | nt | rt | rt |

 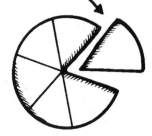  

pa ____s   **pa _____**   **pai _____**   **passpo _____**

Five-a-Day: Add and Subtract to 18

Solve.	Solve.	Solve.
$15 - 9 =$ _____	$12 + 3 =$ _____	$15 - 6 =$ _____
$13 - 6 =$ _____	$13 - 9 =$ _____	$13 + 5 =$ _____

There were 13 aphids on Lucas' roses. He brushed 8 of them off. How many aphids were left?	Jonas planted 18 flowers in his yard. The grasshoppers ate 9 of them. How many flowers does Jonas have left?
There were _____ aphids left.	Jonas has _____ flowers left.

Sentence-a-Day

what   does   ladybugs   like   to   eat

- -

Write the correct digraph at the end of each word.

    ch   sh   sh   th

wren ____   **toothbru** ____   **wrea** ____   **tra** ____

         © Teacher Created Materials, Inc.

Page 5

Name _____ Practice 1

Five-a-Day: Numbers to 10

Draw 1 heart. | Draw 2 cookies. | Draw 3 balloons.
Draw 4 happy faces. | Draw 5 circles.

Sentence-a-Day

i   like   bears

I like bears.

About Me!

My first name is _Jenny_ .

My last name is _Chao_ .

I am _7_ years old.

© Teacher Created Materials, Inc.   5   #2514 Daily Skills Practice

Page 6

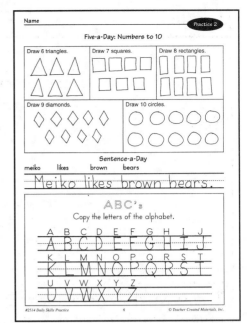

Name _____ Practice 2

Five-a-Day: Numbers to 10

Draw 6 triangles. | Draw 7 squares. | Draw 8 rectangles.
Draw 9 diamonds. | Draw 10 circles.

Sentence-a-Day

meiko   likes   brown   bears

Meiko likes brown bears.

ABC's
Copy the letters of the alphabet.

A B C D E F G H I J
ABCDEFGHIJ
K L M N O P Q R S T
KLMNOPQRST
U V W X Y Z
UVWXYZ

#2514 Daily Skills Practice   6   © Teacher Created Materials, Inc.

Page 7

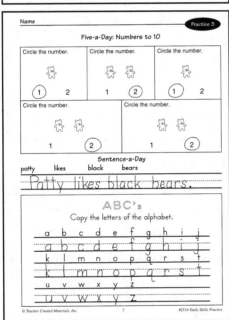

Name _____ Practice 3

Five-a-Day: Numbers to 10

Circle the number. | Circle the number. | Circle the number.
(1) 2 | 1 (2) | (1) 2
Circle the number. | Circle the number.
1 (2) | 1 (2)

Sentence-a-Day

patty   likes   black   bears

Patty likes black bears.

ABC's
Copy the letters of the alphabet.

a b c d e f g h i j
abcdefghij
k l m n o p q r s t
klmnopqrst
u v w x y z
uvwxyz

© Teacher Created Materials, Inc.   7   #2514 Daily Skills Practice

Page 8

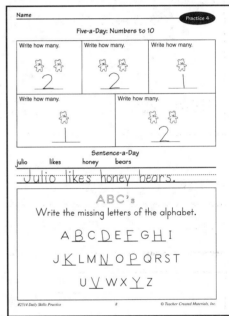

Name _____ Practice 4

Five-a-Day: Numbers to 10

Write how many. | Write how many. | Write how many.
2 | 2 | 1
Write how many. | Write how many.
1 | 2

Sentence-a-Day

julio   likes   honey   bears

Julio likes honey bears.

ABC's
Write the missing letters of the alphabet.

A _B_ C D _E_ F G H I
J _K_ L M N _O_ P Q R S T
U _V_ W X _Y_ Z

#2514 Daily Skills Practice   8   © Teacher Created Materials, Inc.

Page 9

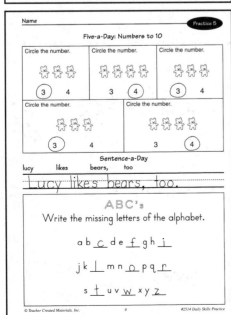

Name _____ Practice 5

Five-a-Day: Numbers to 10

Circle the number. | Circle the number. | Circle the number.
(3) 4 | 3 (4) | (3) 4
Circle the number. | Circle the number.
(3) 4 | 3 (4)

Sentence-a-Day

lucy   likes   bears,   too

Lucy likes bears, too.

ABC's
Write the missing letters of the alphabet.

a b _c_ d e _f_ g h _i_
j k _l_ m n _o_ p q r
s _t_ u v _w_ x y z

© Teacher Created Materials, Inc.   9   #2514 Daily Skills Practice

Page 10

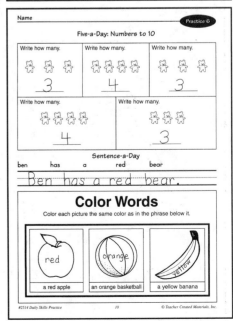

Name _____ Practice 6

Five-a-Day: Numbers to 10

Write how many. | Write how many. | Write how many.
3 | 4 | 3
Write how many. | Write how many.
4 | 3

Sentence-a-Day

ben   has   a   red   bear

Ben has a red bear.

Color Words
Color each picture the same color as in the phrase below it.

red | orange | yellow
a red apple | an orange basketball | a yellow banana

#2514 Daily Skills Practice   10   © Teacher Created Materials, Inc.

Page 11

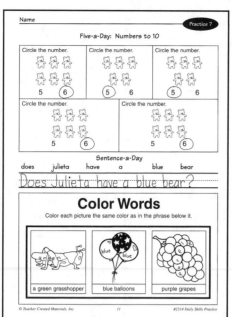

Page 12

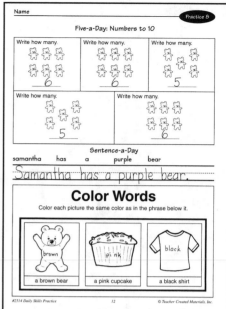

Page 13

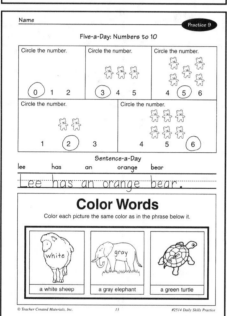

Page 14

Page 15

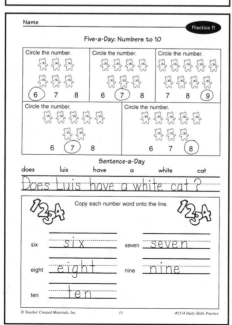

Page 16

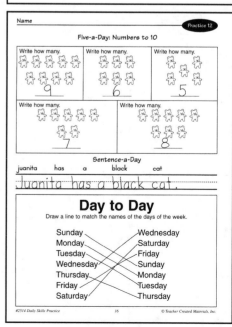

Page 17

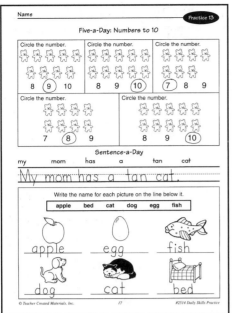

Page 18

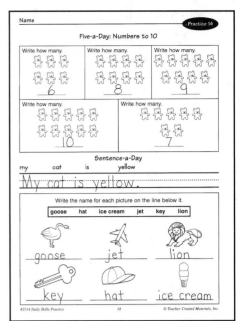

Page 19

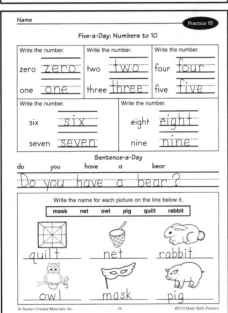

Page 20

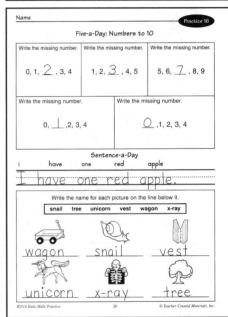

Page 21

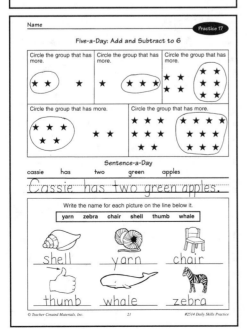

Page 22

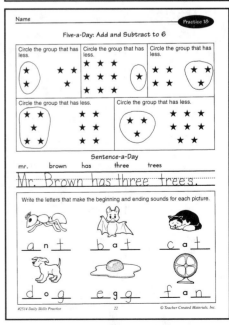

Page 23

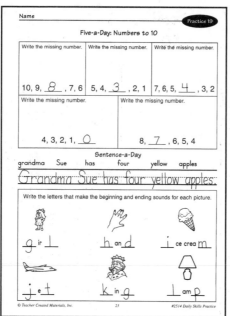

Page 24

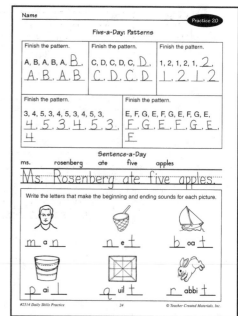

Page 25

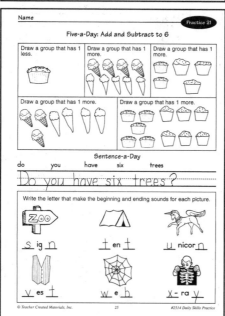

Page 26

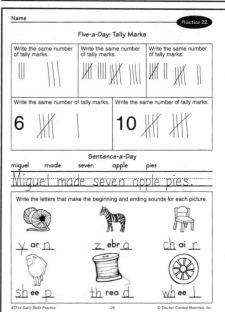

Page 27

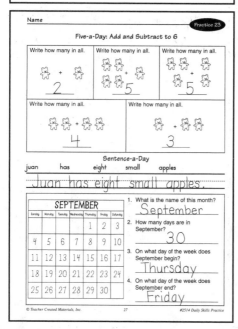

Page 28

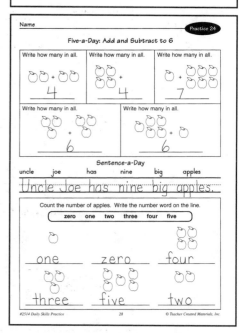

Page 29

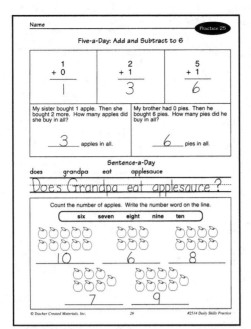

Page 30

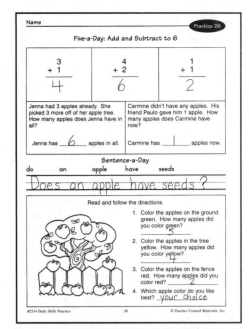

Page 31

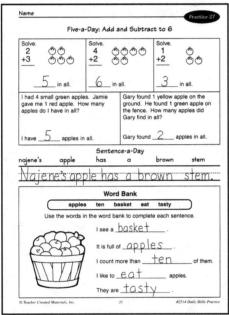

Page 32

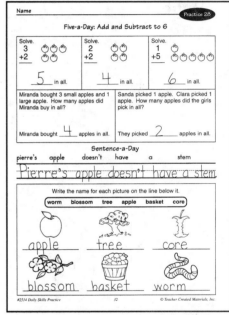

Page 33

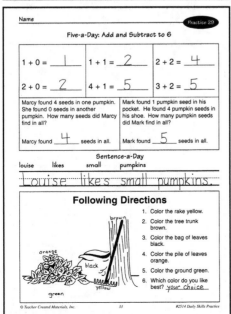

Page 34

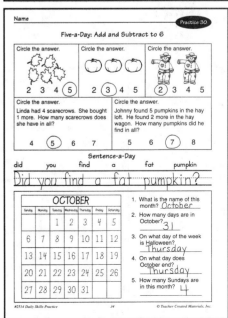

Page 35

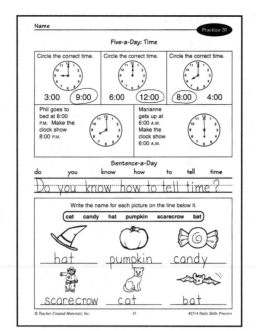

Page 36

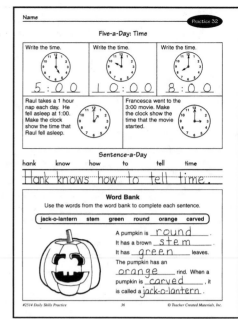

Page 37

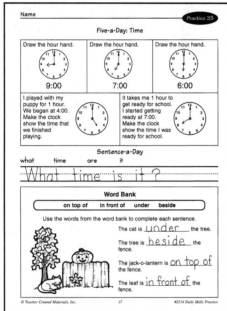

Page 38

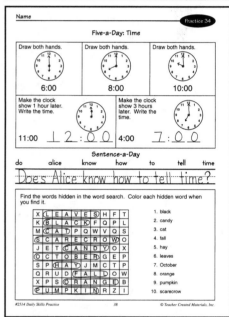

Page 39

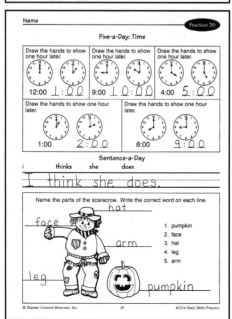

Page 40

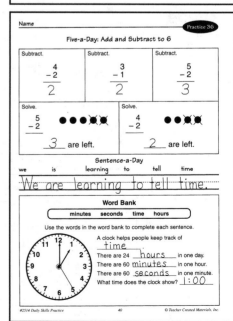

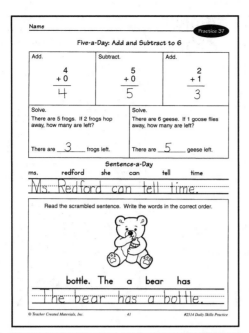

Name _____

Practice 37

Five-a-Day: Add and Subtract to 6

Add.	Subtract.	Add.
4 + 0 —— 4	5 – 0 —— 5	2 + 1 —— 3

Solve.	Solve.
There are 5 frogs. If 2 frogs hop away, how many are left? There are __3__ frogs left.	There are 6 geese. If 1 goose flies away, how many are left? There are __5__ geese left.

Sentence-a-Day

ms.   redford   she   can   tell   time

Ms. Redford can tell time.

Read the scrambled sentence. Write the words in the correct order.

bottle.   The   a   bear   has

The bear has a bottle.

© Teacher Created Materials, Inc.   41   #2514 Daily Skills Practice

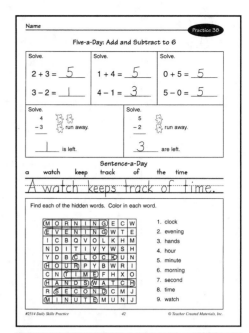

Name _____

Practice 38

Five-a-Day: Add and Subtract to 6

Solve.	Solve.	Solve.
2 + 3 = __5__ 3 – 2 = __1__	1 + 4 = __5__ 4 – 1 = __3__	0 + 5 = __5__ 5 – 0 = __5__

Solve.	Solve.
4 – 3 —— run away. __1__ is left.	5 – 2 —— run away. __3__ are left.

Sentence-a-Day

a   watch   keep   track   of   the   time

A watch keeps track of time.

Find each of the hidden words. Color in each word.

M	O	R	N	I	N	G	E	C	W
E	V	E	N	I	N	G	W	T	E
I	C	B	Q	V	O	L	K	H	M
N	D	I	T	I	V	Y	W	S	H
Y	D	B	C	L	O	C	K	U	N
H	O	U	R	P	Y	B	W	R	I
C	N	T	I	M	E	F	H	X	O
H	A	N	D	S	W	A	T	C	H
R	S	E	C	O	N	D	C	M	J
M	I	N	U	T	E	M	U	N	J

1. clock
2. evening
3. hands
4. hour
5. minute
6. morning
7. second
8. time
9. watch

#2514 Daily Skills Practice   42   © Teacher Created Materials, Inc.

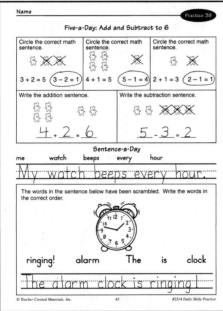

Name _____

Practice 39

Five-a-Day: Add and Subtract to 6

Circle the correct math sentence.	Circle the correct math sentence.	Circle the correct math sentence.
3 + 2 = 5 (3 – 2 = 1)	4 + 1 = 5 (5 – 1 = 4)	2 + 1 = 3 (2 – 1 = 1)

Write the addition sentence.	Write the subtraction sentence.
4 + 2 = 6	5 – 3 = 2

Sentence-a-Day

me   watch   beeps   every   hour

My watch beeps every hour.

The words in the sentence below have been scrambled. Write the words in the correct order.

ringing!   alarm   The   is   clock

The alarm clock is ringing!

© Teacher Created Materials, Inc.   43   #2514 Daily Skills Practice

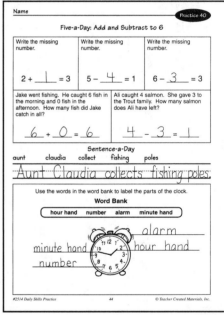

Name _____

Practice 40

Five-a-Day: Add and Subtract to 6

Write the missing number.	Write the missing number.	Write the missing number.
2 + __1__ = 3	5 – __4__ = 1	6 – __3__ = 3

Jake went fishing. He caught 6 fish in the morning and 0 fish in the afternoon. How many fish did Jake catch in all? 6 + 0 = 6	Ali caught 4 salmon. She gave 3 to the Trout family. How many salmon does Ali have left? 4 – 3 = 1

Sentence-a-Day

aunt   claudia   collect   fishing   poles

Aunt Claudia collects fishing poles.

Use the words in the word bank to label the parts of the clock.

Word Bank

| hour hand | number | alarm | minute hand |

alarm
minute hand   hour hand
number

#2514 Daily Skills Practice   44   © Teacher Created Materials, Inc.

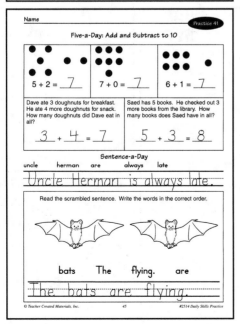

Name _____

Practice 41

Five-a-Day: Add and Subtract to 10

5 + 2 = __7__	7 + 0 = __7__	6 + 1 = __7__

Dave ate 3 doughnuts for breakfast. He ate 4 more doughnuts for snack. How many doughnuts did Dave eat in all? 3 + 4 = 7	Saed has 5 books. He checked out 3 more books from the library. How many books does Saed have in all? 5 + 3 = 8

Sentence-a-Day

uncle   herman   are   always   late

Uncle Herman is always late.

Read the scrambled sentence. Write the words in the correct order.

bats   The   flying.   are

The bats are flying.

© Teacher Created Materials, Inc.   45   #2514 Daily Skills Practice

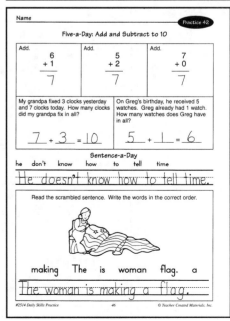

Name _____

Practice 42

Five-a-Day: Add and Subtract to 10

Add.	Add.	Add.
6 + 1 —— 7	5 + 2 —— 7	7 + 0 —— 7

My grandpa fixed 3 clocks yesterday and 7 clocks today. How many clocks did my grandpa fix in all? 7 + 3 = 10	On Greg's birthday, he received 5 watches. Greg already had 1 watch. How many watches does Greg have in all? 5 + 1 = 6

Sentence-a-Day

he   don't   know   how   to   tell   time

He doesn't know how to tell time.

Read the scrambled sentence. Write the words in the correct order.

making   The   is   woman   flag.   a

The woman is making a flag.

#2514 Daily Skills Practice   46   © Teacher Created Materials, Inc.

Page 47

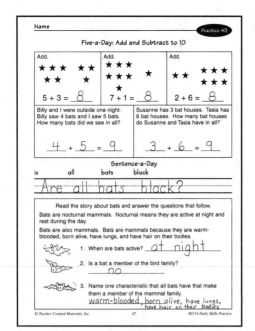

Practice 43

Five-a-Day: Add and Subtract to 10

Add.	Add.	Add.
★★★ ★★ ★★ ★ 5 + 3 = 8	★★★ ★★★ ★ ★ 7 + 1 = 8	★★ ★★★ ★★★ 2 + 6 = 8

Billy and I were outside one night. Billy had 4 bats and I saw 5 bats. How many bats did we see in all? 4 + 5 = 9	Susanne has 3 bat houses. Tasia has 6 bat houses. How many bat houses do Susanne and Tasia have in all? 3 + 6 = 9

Sentence-a-Day

is   all   bats   black

Are all bats black?

Read the story about bats and answer the questions that follow.

Bats are nocturnal mammals. Nocturnal means they are active at night and rest during the day.

Bats are also mammals. Bats are mammals because they are warm-blooded, born alive, have lungs, and have hair on their bodies.

1. When are bats active? at night

2. Is a bat a member of the bird family? no

3. Name one characteristic that all bats have that make them a member of the mammal family. warm-blooded, born alive, have lungs, have hair on their bodies

© Teacher Created Materials, Inc. — 47 — #2514 Daily Skills Practice

---

Page 48

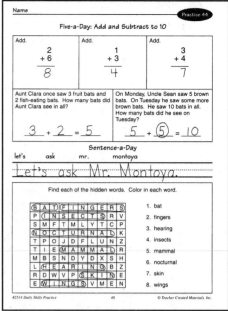

Name _____

Practice 44

Five-a-Day: Add and Subtract to 10

Add.	Add.	Add.
2 + 6 8	1 + 3 4	3 + 4 7

Aunt Clara once saw 3 fruit bats and 2 fish-eating bats. How many bats did Aunt Clara see in all? 3 + 2 = 5	On Monday, Uncle Sean saw 5 brown bats. On Tuesday he saw some more brown bats. He saw 10 bats in all. How many bats did he see on Tuesday? 5 + ⑤ = 10

Sentence-a-Day

let's   ask   mr.   montoya

Let's ask Mr. Montoya.

Find each of the hidden words. Color in each word.

B	A	T	F	I	N	G	E	R	S
P	I	N	S	E	C	T	S	R	V
S	M	F	T	M	L	Y	T	C	P
N	O	C	T	U	R	N	A	L	K
T	P	O	J	D	F	L	U	N	Z
T	I	E	M	A	M	M	A	L	R
M	B	S	N	D	Y	D	X	S	H
L	H	E	A	R	I	N	G	B	Z
R	D	W	V	P	S	K	I	N	E
E	W	I	N	G	S	V	M	E	N

1. bat
2. fingers
3. hearing
4. insects
5. mammal
6. nocturnal
7. skin
8. wings

#2514 Daily Skills Practice — 48 — © Teacher Created Materials, Inc.

Page 49

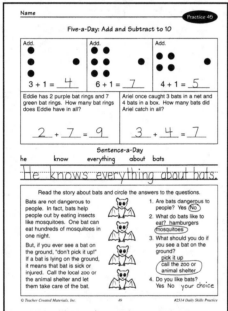

Name _____

Practice 45

Five-a-Day: Add and Subtract to 10

Add.	Add.	Add.
● ● ● 3 + 1 = 4	● ● ● ● ● ● ● 6 + 1 = 7	● ● ● ● ● 4 + 1 = 5

Eddie has 2 purple bat rings and 7 green bat rings. How many bat rings does Eddie have in all? 2 + 7 = 9	Ariel once caught 3 bats in a net and 4 bats in a box. How many bats did Ariel catch in all? 3 + 4 = 7

Sentence-a-Day

he   know   everything   about   bats

He knows everything about bats.

Read the story about bats and circle the answers to the questions.

Bats are not dangerous to people. In fact, bats help people out by eating insects like mosquitoes. One bat can eat hundreds of mosquitoes in one night.

But, if you ever see a bat on the ground, "don't pick it up!" If a bat is lying on the ground, it means that bat is sick or injured. Call the local zoo or the animal shelter and let them take care of the bat.

1. Are bats dangerous to people? Yes (No)
2. What do bats like to eat? hamburgers (mosquitoes)
3. What should you do if you see a bat on the ground? pick it up (call the zoo or animal shelter)
4. Do you like bats? Yes No your choice

© Teacher Created Materials, Inc. — 49 — #2514 Daily Skills Practice

---

Page 50

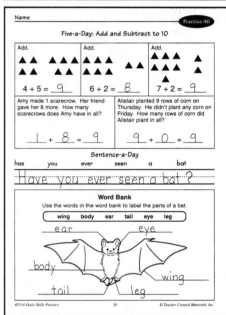

Name _____

Practice 46

Five-a-Day: Add and Subtract to 10

Add.	Add.	Add.
▲▲ ▲▲▲ ▲▲ ▲▲ 4 + 5 = 9	▲▲▲ ▲▲ ▲ 6 + 2 = 8	▲▲▲ ▲ ▲▲▲ ▲ 7 + 2 = 9

Amy made 1 scarecrow. Her friend gave her 8 more. How many scarecrows does Amy have in all? 1 + 8 = 9	Alistair planted 9 rows of corn on Thursday. He didn't plant any corn on Friday. How many rows of corn did Alistair plant in all? 9 + 0 = 9

Sentence-a-Day

has   you   ever   seen   a   bat

Have you ever seen a bat?

Word Bank

Use the words in the word bank to label the parts of a bat.

wing   body   ear   tail   eye   leg

ear   eye
body   wing
tail   leg

#2514 Daily Skills Practice — 50 — © Teacher Created Materials, Inc.

Page 51

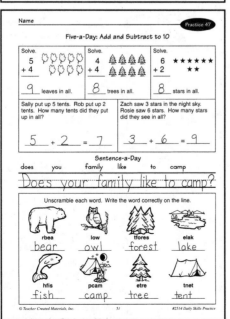

Name _____

Practice 47

Five-a-Day: Add and Subtract to 10

Solve.	Solve.	Solve.
5 + 4 9 leaves in all.	4 + 4 8 trees in all.	6 + 2 8 stars in all.

Sally put up 5 tents. Rob put up 2 tents. How many tents did they put up in all? 5 + 2 = 7	Zach saw 3 stars in the night sky. Rosie saw 6 stars. How many stars did they see in all? 3 + 6 = 9

Sentence-a-Day

does   you   family   like   to   camp

Does your family like to camp?

Unscramble each word. Write the word correctly on the line.

rbea	low	tfores	elak
bear	owl	forest	lake

hfis	pcam	etre	tnet
fish	camp	tree	tent

© Teacher Created Materials, Inc. — 51 — #2514 Daily Skills Practice

---

Page 52

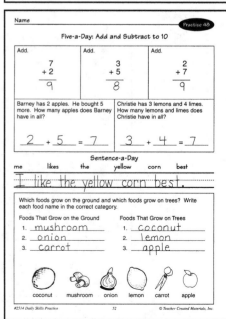

Name _____

Practice 48

Five-a-Day: Add and Subtract to 10

Add.	Add.	Add.
7 + 2 9	3 + 5 8	2 + 7 9

Barney has 2 apples. He bought 5 more. How many apples does Barney have in all? 2 + 5 = 7	Christie has 3 lemons and 4 limes. How many lemons and limes does Christie have in all? 3 + 4 = 7

Sentence-a-Day

me   likes   the   yellow   corn   best

I like the yellow corn best.

Which foods grow on the ground and which foods grow on trees? Write each food name in the correct category.

Foods That Grow on the Ground
1. mushroom
2. onion
3. carrot

Foods That Grow on Trees
1. coconut
2. lemon
3. apple

coconut   mushroom   onion   lemon   carrot   apple

#2514 Daily Skills Practice — 52 — © Teacher Created Materials, Inc.

Name _____ Practice 49

Five-a-Day: Add and Subtract to 10

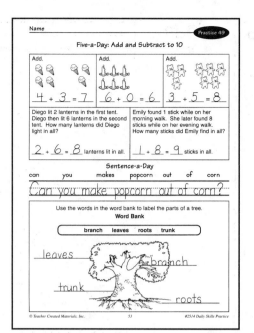

Add.	Add.	Add.
$4 + 3 = 7$	$6 + 0 = 6$	$3 + 5 = 8$

Diego lit 2 lanterns in the first tent. Diego then lit 6 lanterns in the second tent. How many lanterns did Diego light in all?

$2 + 6 = 8$ lanterns lit in all.

Emily found 1 stick while on her morning walk. She later found 8 sticks while on her evening walk. How many sticks did Emily find in all?

$1 + 8 = 9$ sticks in all.

Sentence-a-Day

can   you   makes   popcorn   out   of   corn

Can you make popcorn out of corn?

Use the words in the word bank to label the parts of a tree.

Word Bank

branch   leaves   roots   trunk

leaves   branch   trunk   roots

53   #2514 Daily Skills Practice

Name _____ Practice 50

Five-a-Day: Add and Subtract to 10

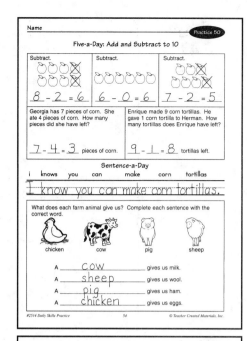

Subtract.	Subtract.	Subtract.
$8 - 2 = 6$	$6 - 0 = 6$	$7 - 2 = 5$

Georgia has 7 pieces of corn. She ate 4 pieces of corn. How many pieces did she have left?

$7 - 4 = 3$ pieces of corn.

Enrique made 9 corn tortillas. He gave 1 corn tortilla to Herman. How many tortillas does Enrique have left?

$9 - 1 = 8$ tortillas left.

Sentence-a-Day

i   knows   you   can   make   corn   tortillas

I know you can make corn tortillas.

What does each farm animal give us? Complete each sentence with the correct word.

chicken   cow   pig   sheep

A cow gives us milk.

A sheep gives us wool.

A pig gives us ham.

A chicken gives us eggs.

#2514 Daily Skills Practice   54

Name _____ Practice 51

Five-a-Day: Add and Subtract to 10

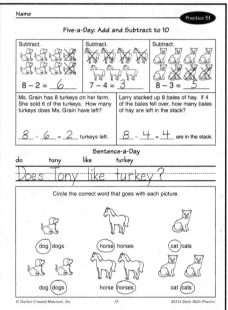

Subtract.	Subtract.	Subtract.
$8 - 2 = 6$	$7 - 4 = 3$	$8 - 3 = 5$

Ms. Grain has 8 turkeys on her farm. She sold 6 of the turkeys. How many turkeys does Ms. Grain have left?

$8 - 6 = 2$ turkeys left.

Larry stacked up 8 bales of hay. If 4 of the bales fell over, how many bales of hay are left in the stack?

$8 - 4 = 4$ are in the stack.

Sentence-a-Day

do   tony   like   turkey

Does Tony like turkey?

Circle the correct word that goes with each picture.

dog (dogs)   horse (horses)   cat (cats)

dog (dogs)   horse (horses)   cat (cats)

55   #2514 Daily Skills Practice

Name _____ Practice 52

Five-a-Day: Add and Subtract to 10

Subtract.	Subtract.	Subtract.
$9 - 3 = 6$	$7 - 2 = 5$	$6 - 4 = 2$

There were 9 children playing outside. If 8 children went inside, how many children stayed outside playing?

$9 - 8 = 1$ child.

Mom placed 8 pumpkin pies were sitting on the window sill. The dog ate 4 of them. How many pies are left?

$8 - 4 = 4$ pies were left.

Sentence-a-Day

jay   think   a   spider   has   eight   legs

Jay thinks a spider has eight legs.

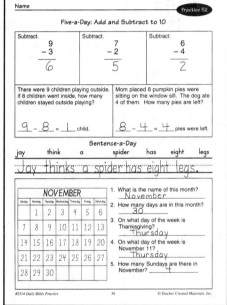

NOVEMBER						
Sunday	Monday	Tuesday	Wednesday	Thursday	Friday	Saturday
		1	2	3	4	5	6
7	8	9	10	11	12	13
14	15	16	17	18	19	20
21	22	23	24	25	26	27
28	29	30				

1. What is the name of this month?
   November
2. How many days are in this month?
   30
3. On what day of the week is Thanksgiving?
   Thursday
4. On what day of the week is November 11?
   Thursday
5. How many Sundays are there in November? 4

#2514 Daily Skills Practice   56

Name _____ Practice 53

Five-a-Day: Add and Subtract to 10

Subtract.	Subtract.	Subtract.
$6 - 3 = 3$	$7 - 5 = 2$	$3 - 2 = 1$

Uncle Roberto made 1 cornucopia. He sold it. How many cornucopias does Uncle Roberto have left?

$1 - 1 = 0$ cornucopia.

Soua made 4 pumpkin pies for her family. Soua's family ate 2 pumpkin pies. How many pumpkin pies does Soua have left?

$4 - 2 = 2$ pies left.

Sentence-a-Day

mr.   vang   made   a   turkey   dinner

Mr. Vang made a turkey dinner.

Write the name for each picture on the line below it.

corn   Pilgrim   Indian   turkey   Mayflower   pie

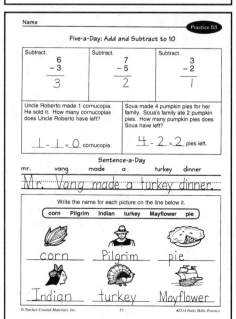

corn   Pilgrim   pie

Indian   turkey   Mayflower

57   #2514 Daily Skills Practice

Name _____ Practice 54

Five-a-Day: Add and Subtract to 10

Subtract.	Subtract.	Subtract.
$8 - 1 = 7$	$2 - 2 = 0$	$4 - 2 = 2$

Nekesha collects feathers. Yesterday she collected 7 yellow feathers. She dropped 4 of them on her way home. How many feathers does Nekesha have left?

$7 - 4 = 3$ feathers left.

Omar saw 7 turkeys sitting on the gate. If 3 of the turkeys flew away, how many turkeys were left?

$7 - 3 = 4$ turkeys left.

Sentence-a-Day

ms.   yang's   turkey   it   makes   lot   of   noise

Ms. Yang's turkey makes lots of noise.

Thanksgiving Dinner

Use the words from the word bank to label each part of the picture.

Word Bank

table   chair   candle   dinner   place mat

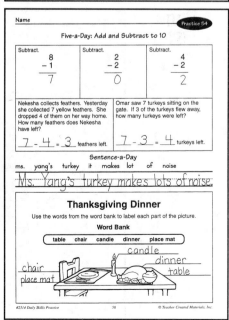

candle   dinner   table   chair   place mat

#2514 Daily Skills Practice   58

Page 59

Page 60

Page 61

Page 62

Page 63

Page 64

Page 59

Name _____ Practice 55

Five-a-Day: Add and Subtract to 10

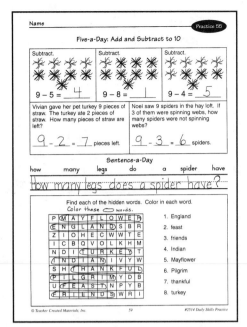

Subtract. $9 - 5 = 4$

Subtract. $9 - 8 = 1$

Subtract. $9 - 4 = 5$

Vivian gave her pet turkey 9 pieces of straw. The turkey ate 2 pieces of straw. How many pieces of straw are left?

$9 - 2 = 7$ pieces left.

Noel saw 9 spiders in the hay loft. If 3 of them were spinning webs, how many spiders were not spinning webs?

$9 - 3 = 6$ spiders.

Sentence-a-Day

how   many   legs   do   a   spider   have

How many legs does a spider have?

Find each of the hidden words. Color in each word.
Color these ⬭ words.

P	M	A	Y	F	L	O	W	E	R
E	N	G	L	A	N	D	S	B	R
Z	I	O	H	E	C	W	W	T	E
I	C	B	Q	V	O	L	K	H	M
N	D	I	T	U	R	K	E	Y	T
I	N	D	I	A	N	I	V	Y	W
S	H	T	H	A	N	K	F	U	L
P	I	L	G	R	I	M	Y	D	B
U	F	E	A	S	T	N	P	Y	B
F	R	I	E	N	D	S	W	R	I

1. England
2. feast
3. friends
4. Indian
5. Mayflower
6. Pilgrim
7. thankful
8. turkey

© Teacher Created Materials, Inc.   59   #2514 Daily Skills Practice

Page 60

Name _____ Practice 56

Five-a-Day: Add and Subtract to 10

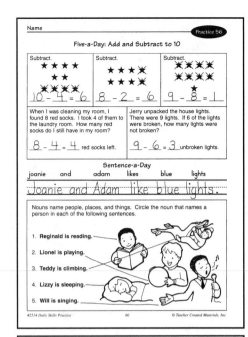

Subtract. $10 - 4 = 6$

Subtract. $8 - 2 = 6$

Subtract. $9 - 8 = 1$

When I was cleaning my room, I found 8 red socks. I took 4 of them to the laundry room. How many red socks do I still have in my room?

$8 - 4 = 4$ red socks left.

Jerry unpacked the house lights. There were 9 lights. If 6 of the lights were broken, how many lights were not broken?

$9 - 6 = 3$ unbroken lights.

Sentence-a-Day

joanie   and   adam   likes   blue   lights

Joanie and Adam like blue lights.

Nouns name people, places, and things. Circle the noun that names a person in each of the following sentences.

1. Reginald is reading.
2. Lionel is playing.
3. Teddy is climbing.
4. Lizzy is sleeping.
5. Will is singing.

#2514 Daily Skills Practice   60   © Teacher Created Materials, Inc.

Page 61

Name _____ Practice 57

Five-a-Day: Add and Subtract to 10

Add.
$3 + 2 = 5$
$2 + 3 = 5$

Subtract.
$5 - 3 = 2$
$5 - 2 = 3$

Add.
$6 + 2 = 8$
$2 + 6 = 8$

Timmy had 8 green marbles. He gave 6 marbles to his friend Mateo. How many marbles does Timmy have left?

$8 - 6 = 2$ marbles left.

Jessie bought 2 stickers. Her father gave her some stickers. Now Jessie has 6 stickers in all. How many stickers did her father give her?

$2 + 4 = 6$ stickers in all.

Sentence-a-Day

they   singed   a   song   about   lights

They sang a song about lights.

Nouns name people, places, and things. Circle the noun that names a thing in each of the following sentences.

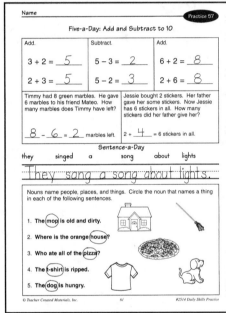

1. The mop is old and dirty.
2. Where is the orange house?
3. Who ate all of the pizza?
4. The t-shirt is ripped.
5. The dog is hungry.

© Teacher Created Materials, Inc.   61   #2514 Daily Skills Practice

Page 62

Name _____ Practice 58

Five-a-Day: Add and Subtract to 10

Solve.
$7 + 2$
9 in all.

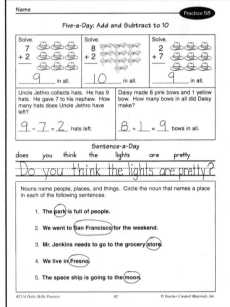

Solve.
$8 + 2$
10 in all.

Solve.
$2 + 7$
9 in all.

Uncle Jethro collects hats. He has 9 hats. He gave 7 to his nephew. How many hats does Uncle Jethro have left?

$9 - 7 = 2$ hats left.

Daisy made 8 pink bows and 1 yellow bow. How many bows in all did Daisy make?

$8 + 1 = 9$ bows in all.

Sentence-a-Day

does   you   think   the   lights   are   pretty

Do you think the lights are pretty?

Nouns name people, places, and things. Circle the noun that names a place in each of the following sentences.

1. The park is full of people.
2. We went to San Francisco for the weekend.
3. Mr. Jenkins needs to go to the grocery store.
4. We live in Fresno.
5. The space ship is going to the moon.

#2514 Daily Skills Practice   62   © Teacher Created Materials, Inc.

Page 63

Name _____ Practice 59

Five-a-Day: Add and Subtract to 10

Solve.
$3 + 2 = 5$
$2 + 3 = 5$

Solve.
$2 + 4 = 6$
$4 + 2 = 6$

Solve.
$0 + 7 = 7$
$7 + 0 = 7$

My grandma made 4 fruit cakes. My mother made 5 fruit cakes. How many fruit cakes did they make in all?

$4 + 5 = 9$ fruit cakes.

My dad baked 5 hams. My grandpa baked 4 hams. How many hams did they bake in all?

$5 + 4 = 9$ hams in all.

Sentence-a-Day

mark   and   martin   was   chasing   a   turkey

Mark and Martin were chasing a turkey.

Use one of these nouns to complete each sentence.

| Shelly | home | Main Street | Herman | popcorn |

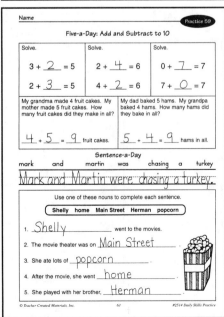

1. Shelly _____ went to the movies.
2. The movie theater was on Main Street.
3. She ate lots of popcorn.
4. After the movie, she went home.
5. She played with her brother, Herman.

© Teacher Created Materials, Inc.   63   #2514 Daily Skills Practice

Page 64

Name _____ Practice 60

Five-a-Day: Add and Subtract to 10

Circle the correct answer.
$8 - 4 =$
3   (4)   5

Circle the correct answer.
$3 + 0 =$
0   1   2   (3)

Circle the correct answer.
$8 - \_\_ = 3$
4   (5)   6   7

Suzy gathered 2 orange leaves. Then she gathered some brown leaves. She now has 7 leaves in all. How many brown leaves did she gather?

$2 + 5 = 7$

Brad picked several small poinsettias. He picked 2 large poinsettias. He now has 5 poinsettias. How many small poinsettias did Brad pick?

$3 + 2 = 5$

Sentence-a-Day

is   roses   red   or   green

Are roses red or green?

Use one of these nouns to complete each sentence.

| paper | Walker | shoes | dinner | shoe store |

1. Mr. Walker went to work.
2. He works at a shoe store.
3. He sells shoes.
4. When he returns home, he likes to read the paper.
5. Mr. Walker then eats dinner.

#2514 Daily Skills Practice   64   © Teacher Created Materials, Inc.

Page 65

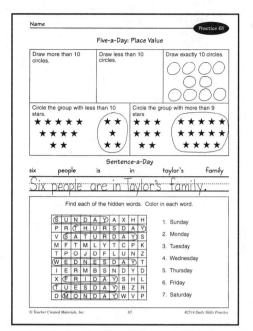

Page 66

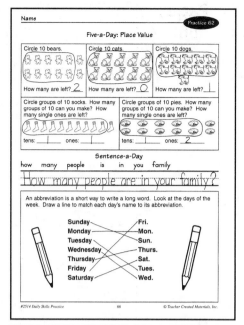

Page 67

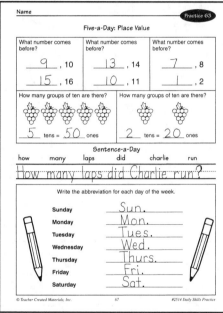

Page 68

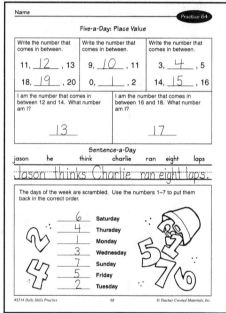

Page 69

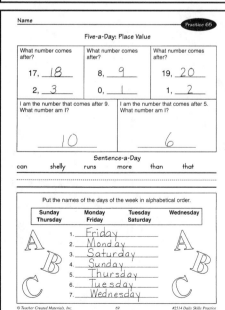

Page 70

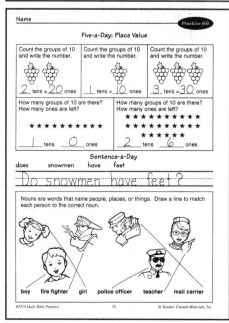

Page 71

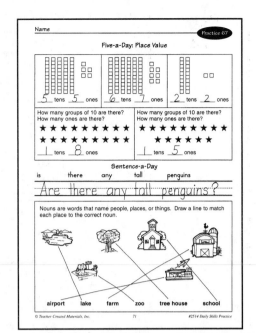

Page 72

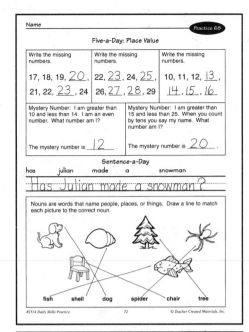

Page 73

Page 74

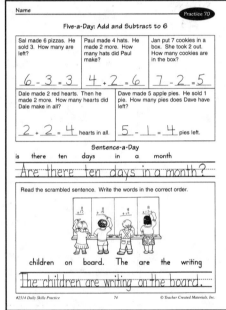

Page 75

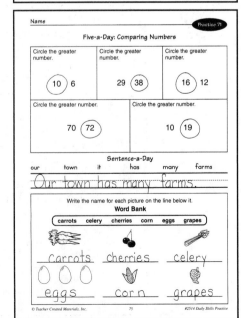

Page 76

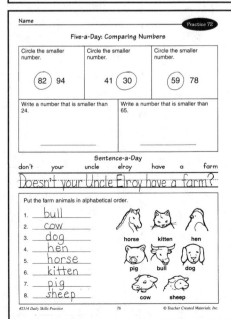

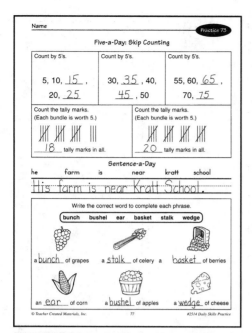

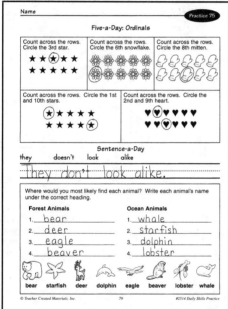

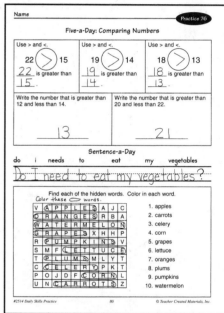

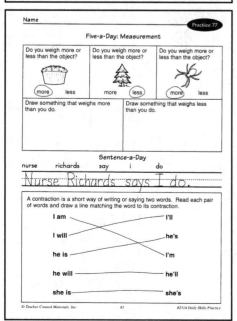

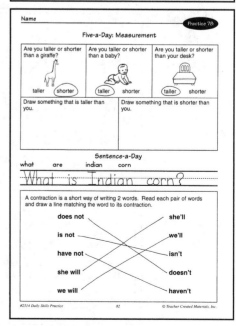

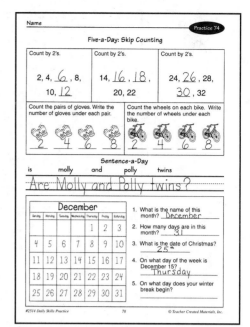

Page 83

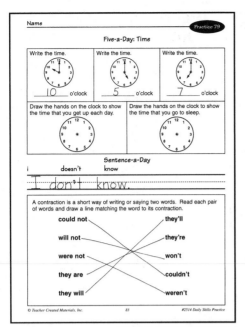

Page 84

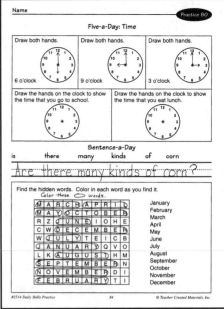

Page 85

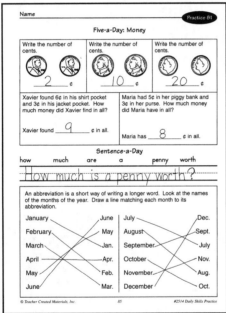

Page 86

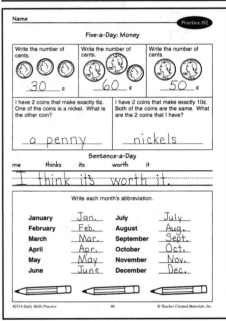

Page 87

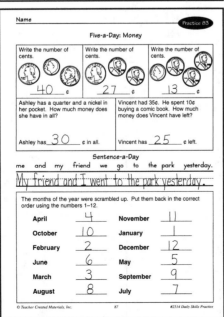

Page 88

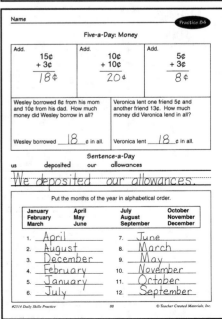

Page 89

Practice 85

Five-a-Day: Money

Subtract.	Subtract.	Subtract.
17¢ − 10¢ **7¢**	25¢ − 13¢ **12¢**	13¢ − 11¢ **2¢**

Stephanie had 18¢. She spent 10¢ on an ice cream cone. How much money does Stephanie have left?	Tyrone had 36¢. He bought a model car for 25¢. How much money does Tyrone have left?
Stephanie has **8** ¢ left.	Tyrone has **11** ¢ left.

Sentence-a-Day

i   and   jasmine   likes   to   save   our   money

Jasmine and I like to save our money.

Find each hidden word. Color in the word.
Color these ⬭ words.

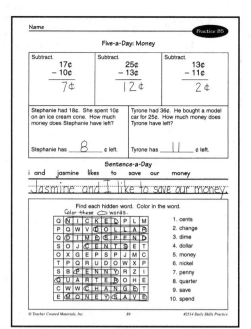

1. cents
2. change
3. dime
4. dollar
5. money
6. nickel
7. penny
8. quarter
9. save
10. spend

89 #2514 Daily Skills Practice

Page 90

Practice 86

Five-a-Day: Money

Write the number of cents.	Write the number of cents.	Write the number of cents.
16	**25**	**55**

Imani had a dime and 2 nickels. How much money did she have in all?	Esperanza had 2 quarters and 1 penny. How much money did she have in all?
Imani had **20** ¢ in all.	Esperanza had **51** ¢ in all.

Sentence-a-Day

me   mom   and   dad   save   they   money,   too

My mom and dad save their money, too.

A compound word is made up of two smaller words.
For example: star + fish = starfish.
Read each pair of words and draw a line to the correct picture of the compound word.

rain + bow =
grand + mother =
fire + fighter =
foot + ball =
tooth + brush =
cup + cake =

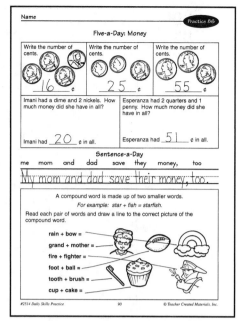

90 © Teacher Created Materials, Inc.

Page 91

Practice 87

Five-a-Day: Money

Write the number of cents.	Write the number of cents.	Write the number of cents.
45 ¢	**75** ¢	**35** ¢

Imogene had 3 dimes. How much money does she have? Does she have enough to buy a 25¢ doll?	Franklin has a quarter, a dime, and a penny. How much money does he have in all? Does he have enough to buy a 50¢ cookie?
Imogene has **30** ¢. (Yes) No	Franklin has **36** ¢. Yes (No)

Sentence-a-Day

they   go   to   the   bank   of   fresno

They go to the Bank of Fresno.

A compound word is made up of two smaller words.
For example: star + fish = starfish.
Read each pair of words and draw a line to the correct picture of the compound word.

ginger + bread =
rain + forest =
jelly + fish =
star + fish =
cheese + burger =

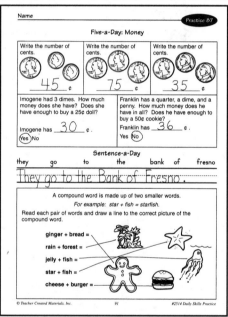

91 #2514 Daily Skills Practice

Page 92

Practice 88

Five-a-Day: Money

Write the number of cents.	Write the number of cents.	Write the number of cents.
30 ¢	**25** ¢	**41** ¢

I have one quarter. How many nickels does it take to make one quarter?	I have one quarter. How many pennies does it take to make one quarter?
It takes **5** nickels to make one quarter.	It takes **25** pennies to make one quarter.

Sentence-a-Day

the   bank   it   is   on   blackstone   avenue

The bank is on Blackstone Avenue.

A compound word is made up of 2 smaller words.
For example: star + fish = starfish.
Read each pair of words and draw a line to the correct picture of the compound word.

type + writer =
sail + boat =
clown + fish =
sea + shell =
candle + light =
basket + ball =

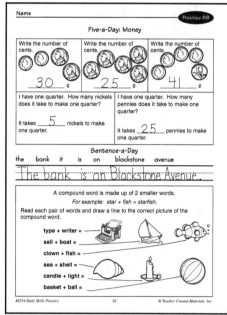

92 © Teacher Created Materials, Inc.

Page 93

Practice 89

Five-a-Day: Measurement

Circle the shortest line.	Circle the shortest line.	Circle the shortest line.

Use counters to measure the length of your paper.	Use counters to measure the length of your pencil.
My paper is _____ counters long.	My pencil is _____ counters long.

Sentence-a-Day

is   neil   the   shortest   boy   at   kratt   school

Is Neil the shortest boy at Kratt School?

Complete each sentence with the correct compound word.

lipstick   butterfly   tablecloth   grasshoppers   cupboard

1. Mr. Thompson put the *tablecloth* on the dinner table.
2. Antoinette put on her mother's *lipstick*.
3. Simon opened the *cupboard* to find that it was empty.
4. Deandre likes to collect *grasshoppers* for his insect collection.
5. A monarch *butterfly* is orange and black.

93 #2514 Daily Skills Practice

Page 94

Practice 90

Five-a-Day: Measurement

Circle the longest line.	Circle the longest line.	Circle the longest line.

Use counters to measure the length of your eraser.	Use counters to measure the length of your crayon.
My eraser is _____ counters long.	My crayon is _____ counters long.

Sentence-a-Day

who   are   the   tallest   person   at   kratt   school

Who is the tallest person at Kratt School?

Complete each sentence with the correct compound word.

newspaper   grandmother   mailbox   doorbell   raincoat

1. My *grandmother* came over to visit.
2. Phil went next door and rang the *doorbell* one time.
3. Shane threw the *newspaper* on the front porch.
4. Samantha dropped the letters in the *mailbox*.
5. Donald carried an umbrella and wore a *raincoat*.

94 © Teacher Created Materials, Inc.

Page 95

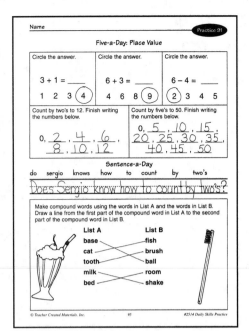

Name _____ Practice 91

Five-a-Day: Place Value

Circle the answer.	Circle the answer.	Circle the answer.
3 + 1 = ____	6 + 3 = ____	6 – 4 = ____
1 2 3 (4)	4 6 8 (9)	(2) 3 4 5

Count by two's to 12. Finish writing the numbers below.	Count by five's to 50. Finish writing the numbers below.
0, _2_, _4_, _6_, _8_, _10_, _12_	0, _5_, _10_, _15_, _20_, _25_, _30_, _35_, _40_, _45_, _50_

Sentence-a-Day

do   sergio   knows   how   to   count   by   two's

Does Sergio know how to count by two's?

Make compound words using the words in List A and the words in List B. Draw a line from the first part of the compound word in List A to the second part of the compound word in List B.

List A   List B
base   fish
cat   brush
tooth   ball
milk   room
bed   shake

© Teacher Created Materials, Inc.   95   #2514 Daily Skills Practice

---

Page 96

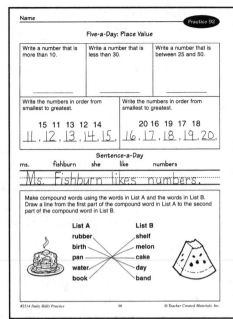

Name _____ Practice 92

Five-a-Day: Place Value

Write a number that is more than 10.	Write a number that is less than 30.	Write a number that is between 25 and 50.

Write the numbers in order from smallest to greatest.	Write the numbers in order from smallest to greatest.
15 11 13 12 14	20 16 19 17 18
11, 12, 13, 14, 15,	16, 17, 18, 19, 20,

Sentence-a-Day

ms.   fishburn   she   like   numbers

Ms. Fishburn likes numbers.

Make compound words using the words in List A and the words in List B. Draw a line from the first part of the compound word in List A to the second part of the compound word in List B.

List A   List B
rubber   shelf
birth   melon
pan   cake
water   day
book   band

#2514 Daily Skills Practice   96   © Teacher Created Materials, Inc.

Page 97

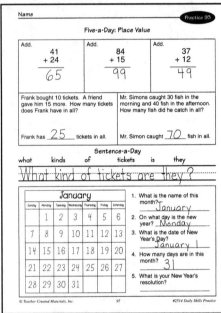

Name _____ Practice 93

Five-a-Day: Place Value

Add.	Add.	Add.
41 + 24 = 65	84 + 15 = 99	37 + 12 = 49

Frank bought 10 tickets. A friend gave him 15 more. How many tickets does Frank have in all?	Mr. Simons caught 30 fish in the morning and 40 fish in the afternoon. How many fish did he catch in all?
Frank has _25_ tickets in all.	Mr. Simon caught _70_ fish in all.

Sentence-a-Day

what   kinds   of   tickets   is   they

What kind of tickets are they?

January

Sunday	Monday	Tuesday	Wednesday	Thursday	Friday	Saturday
		1	2	3	4	5	6
7	8	9	10	11	12	13
14	15	16	17	18	19	20
21	22	23	24	25	26	27
28	29	30	31			

1. What is the name of this month? January
2. On what day is the new year? Monday
3. What is the date of New Year's Day? January 1
4. How many days are in this month? 31
5. What is your New Year's resolution?

© Teacher Created Materials, Inc.   97   #2514 Daily Skills Practice

---

Page 98

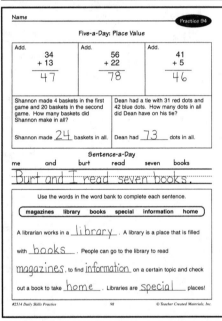

Name _____ Practice 94

Five-a-Day: Place Value

Add.	Add.	Add.
34 + 13 = 47	56 + 22 = 78	41 + 5 = 46

Shannon made 4 baskets in the first game and 20 baskets in the second game. How many baskets did Shannon make in all?	Dean had a tie with 31 red dots and 42 blue dots. How many dots in all did Dean have on his tie?
Shannon made _24_ baskets in all.	Dean had _73_ dots in all.

Sentence-a-Day

me   and   burt   read   seven   books

Burt and I read seven books.

Use the words in the word bank to complete each sentence.

| magazines   library   books   special   information   home |

A librarian works in a _library_. A library is a place that is filled with _books_. People can go to the library to read _magazines_, to find _information_ on a certain topic and check out a book to take _home_. Libraries are _special_ places!

#2514 Daily Skills Practice   98   © Teacher Created Materials, Inc.

Page 99

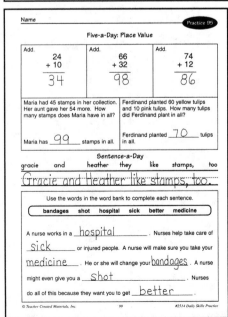

Name _____ Practice 95

Five-a-Day: Place Value

Add.	Add.	Add.
24 + 10 = 34	66 + 32 = 98	74 + 12 = 86

Maria had 45 stamps in her collection. Her aunt gave her 54 more. How many stamps does Maria have in all?	Ferdinand planted 60 yellow tulips and 10 pink tulips. How many tulips did Ferdinand plant in all?
Maria has _99_ stamps in all.	Ferdinand planted _70_ tulips in all.

Sentence-a-Day

gracie   and   heather   they   like   stamps,   too

Gracie and Heather like stamps, too.

Use the words in the word bank to complete each sentence.

| bandages   shot   hospital   sick   better   medicine |

A nurse works in a _hospital_. Nurses help take care of _sick_ or injured people. A nurse will make sure you take your _medicine_. He or she will change your _bandages_. A nurse might even give you a _shot_. Nurses do all of this because they want you to get _better_.

© Teacher Created Materials, Inc.   99   #2514 Daily Skills Practice

---

Page 100

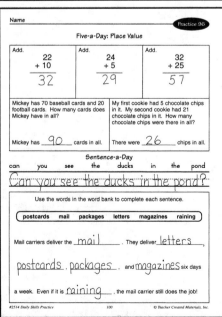

Name _____ Practice 96

Five-a-Day: Place Value

Add.	Add.	Add.
22 + 10 = 32	24 + 5 = 29	32 + 25 = 57

Mickey has 70 baseball cards and 20 football cards. How many cards does Mickey have in all?	My first cookie had 5 chocolate chips in it. My second cookie had 21 chocolate chips in it. How many chocolate chips were there in all?
Mickey has _90_ cards in all.	There were _26_ chips in all.

Sentence-a-Day

can   you   see   the   ducks   in   the   pond

Can you see the ducks in the pond?

Use the words in the word bank to complete each sentence.

| postcards   mail   packages   letters   magazines   raining |

Mail carriers deliver the _mail_. They deliver _letters_, _postcards_, _packages_, and _magazines_ six days a week. Even if it is _raining_, the mail carrier still does the job!

#2514 Daily Skills Practice   100   © Teacher Created Materials, Inc.

Page 101

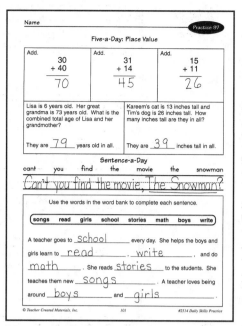

Name

Practice 97

Five-a-Day: Place Value

Add. $30 + 40 = 70$	Add. $31 + 14 = 45$	Add. $15 + 11 = 26$

Lisa is 6 years old. Her great grandma is 73 years old. What is the combined total age of Lisa and her grandmother?

They are __79__ years old in all.

Kareem's cat is 13 inches tall and Tim's dog is 26 inches tall. How many inches tall are they in all?

They are __39__ inches tall in all.

Sentence-a-Day

cant   you   find   the   movie   the   snowman

Can't you find the movie, The Snowman?

Use the words in the word bank to complete each sentence.

songs   read   girls   school   stories   math   boys   write

A teacher goes to __school__ every day. She helps the boys and girls learn to __read__, __write__, and do __math__. She reads __stories__ to the students. She teaches them new __songs__. A teacher loves being around __boys__ and __girls__.

© Teacher Created Materials, Inc.   101   #2514 Daily Skills Practice

---

Page 102

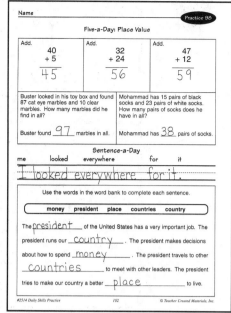

Name

Practice 98

Five-a-Day: Place Value

Add. $40 + 5 = 45$	Add. $32 + 24 = 56$	Add. $47 + 12 = 59$

Buster looked in his toy box and found 87 cat eye marbles and 10 clear marbles. How many marbles did he find in all?

Buster found __97__ marbles in all.

Mohammad has 15 pairs of black socks and 23 pairs of white socks. How many pairs of socks does he have in all?

Mohammad has __38__ pairs of socks.

Sentence-a-Day

me   looked   everywhere   for   it

I looked everywhere for it.

Use the words in the word bank to complete each sentence.

money   president   place   countries   country

The __president__ of the United States has a very important job. The president runs our __country__. The president makes decisions about how to spend __money__. The president travels to other __countries__ to meet with other leaders. The president tries to make our country a better __place__ to live.

#2514 Daily Skills Practice   102   © Teacher Created Materials, Inc.

Page 103

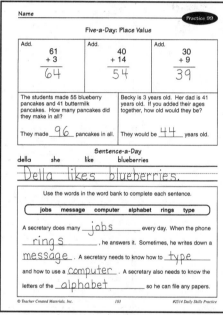

Name

Practice 99

Five-a-Day: Place Value

Add. $61 + 3 = 64$	Add. $40 + 14 = 54$	Add. $30 + 9 = 39$

The students made 55 blueberry pancakes and 41 buttermilk pancakes. How many pancakes did they make in all?

They made __96__ pancakes in all.

Becky is 3 years old. Her dad is 41 years old. If you added their ages together, how old would they be?

They would be __44__ years old.

Sentence-a-Day

della   she   like   blueberries

Della likes blueberries.

Use the words in the word bank to complete each sentence.

jobs   message   computer   alphabet   rings   type

A secretary does many __jobs__ every day. When the phone __rings__, he answers it. Sometimes, he writes down a __message__. A secretary needs to know how to __type__ and how to use a __computer__. A secretary also needs to know the letters of the __alphabet__ so he can file any papers.

© Teacher Created Materials, Inc.   103   #2514 Daily Skills Practice

---

Page 104

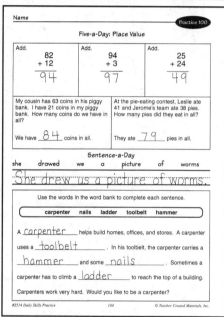

Name

Practice 100

Five-a-Day: Place Value

Add. $82 + 12 = 94$	Add. $94 + 3 = 97$	Add. $25 + 24 = 49$

My cousin has 63 coins in his piggy bank. I have 21 coins in my piggy bank. How many coins do we have in all?

We have __84__ coins in all.

At the pie-eating contest, Leslie ate 41 and Jerome's team ate 38 pies. How many pies did they eat in all?

They ate __79__ pies in all.

Sentence-a-Day

she   drawed   we   a   picture   of   worms

She drew us a picture of worms.

Use the words in the word bank to complete each sentence.

carpenter   nails   ladder   toolbelt   hammer

A __carpenter__ helps build homes, offices, and stores. A carpenter uses a __toolbelt__. In his toolbelt, the carpenter carries a __hammer__ and some __nails__. Sometimes a carpenter has to climb a __ladder__ to reach the top of a building. Carpenters work very hard. Would you like to be a carpenter?

#2514 Daily Skills Practice   104   © Teacher Created Materials, Inc.

Page 105

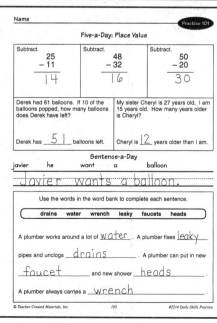

Name

Practice 101

Five-a-Day: Place Value

Subtract. $25 - 11 = 14$	Subtract. $48 - 32 = 16$	Subtract. $50 - 20 = 30$

Derek had 61 balloons. If 10 of the balloons popped, how many balloons does Derek have left?

Derek has __51__ balloons left.

My sister Cheryl is 27 years old. I am 15 years old. How many years older is Cheryl?

Cheryl is __12__ years older than I am.

Sentence-a-Day

javier   he   want   a   balloon

Javier wants a balloon.

Use the words in the word bank to complete each sentence.

drains   water   wrench   leaky   faucets   heads

A plumber works around a lot of __water__. A plumber fixes __leaky__ pipes and unclogs __drains__. A plumber can put in new __faucet__ and new shower __heads__. A plumber always carries a __wrench__.

© Teacher Created Materials, Inc.   105   #2514 Daily Skills Practice

---

Page 106

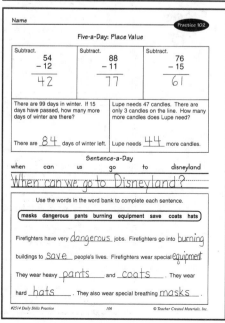

Name

Practice 102

Five-a-Day: Place Value

Subtract. $54 - 12 = 42$	Subtract. $88 - 11 = 77$	Subtract. $76 - 15 = 61$

There are 99 days in winter. If 15 days have passed, how many more days of winter are there?

There are __84__ days of winter left.

Lupe needs 47 candles. There are only 3 candles on the line. How many more candles does Lupe need?

Lupe needs __44__ more candles.

Sentence-a-Day

when   can   us   go   to   disneyland

When can we go to Disneyland?

Use the words in the word bank to complete each sentence.

masks   dangerous   pants   burning   equipment   save   coats   hats

Firefighters have very __dangerous__ jobs. Firefighters go into __burning__ buildings to __save__ people's lives. Firefighters wear special __equipment__. They wear heavy __pants__ and __coats__. They wear hard __hats__. They also wear special breathing __masks__.

#2514 Daily Skills Practice   106   © Teacher Created Materials, Inc.

Page 107

Five-a-Day: Place Value

Subtract.	Subtract.	Subtract.
46 −42 = **4**	38 − 5 = **33**	89 −18 = **71**

There were 64 jelly beans in the jar. Now there are only 22 jelly beans. How many jelly beans are missing?

There are **42** jelly beans missing.

Mary Kaye invited 99 people to the party. Only 30 came. How many people did not come to the party?

69 people did not come to the party.

Sentence-a-Day

why   didnt   you   came   to   the   party

Why didn't you come to the party?

Use the words in the word bank to complete each sentence.

brush   washes   dryer   cut   hairdresser   scissors   color

A **hairdresser** cuts hair. First the hairdresser **washes** your hair.

Then she might **cut** it, give you a permanent, or even

change the **color** of your hair! A hairdresser uses a pair of

scissors, a hair **dryer**, and a hair **brush** to do this job.

© Teacher Created Materials, Inc.   107   #2514 Daily Skills Practice

---

Page 108

Five-a-Day: Place Value

Subtract.	Subtract.	Subtract.
58 −38 = **20**	44 −42 = **2**	95 − 4 = **91**

Jeremy counted 96 stars on Monday and only 26 on Tuesday. How many fewer stars did Jeremy see on Tuesday than on Monday?

Jeremy saw **70** fewer stars.

Leo baked 30 cupcakes for his class. His dog ate 20 of the cupcakes. How many cupcakes does Leo have left?

Leo has **10** cupcakes left.

Sentence-a-Day

why   did   leo   name   his   dog   bandit

Why did Leo name his dog Bandit?

Use the words in the word bank to complete each sentence.

fictional   author   nonfiction   words

An **author** is someone who writes stories for other people to

read. The author might write a **fictional** story. A fictional story is

one the author makes up. An author might write a story that is

nonfiction. Nonfiction means that it is a true story.

A good author needs to know a lot of **words**!

#2514 Daily Skills Practice   108   © Teacher Created Materials, Inc.

Page 109

Five-a-Day: Place Value

Subtract.	Subtract.	Subtract.
23¢ −13¢ = **10¢**	42¢ −12¢ = **30¢**	26¢ −22¢ = **4¢**

Joe had 34¢ in his pocket. If 21¢ fell out of the hole in his pocket, how much money does he have left?

Joe has **13¢** left.

Esmeralda had 95¢ in her lunch bag. She gave her friend 14¢. How much money does she have left in her lunch bag?

Esmeralda has **81¢** left in her lunch bag.

Sentence-a-Day

ryan   he   want   to   buy   a   book

Ryan wants to buy a book.

Adjectives are words that describe a noun (a person, place, or thing). Draw a line matching the picture with the correct adjective and noun phrase. Color the pictures to match each phrase.

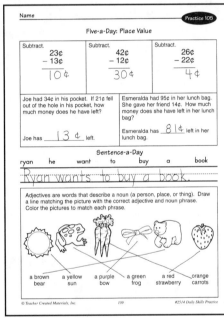

a brown bear   a yellow sun   a purple bow   a green frog   a red strawberry   orange carrots

© Teacher Created Materials, Inc.   109   #2514 Daily Skills Practice

---

Page 110

Five-a-Day: Place Value

Add.	Add.	Add.
30¢ +20¢ = **50¢**	71¢ + 5¢ = **76¢**	31¢ +30¢ = **61¢**

Mia spent 55¢ on popcorn and 20¢ for gum. How much money did Mia spend in all?

Mia spent **75¢** in all.

Elvis bought an eraser for 45¢ and a pencil for 20¢. How much money did Elvis spend in all?

Elvis spent **65¢** in all.

Sentence-a-Day

did   you   like   the   new   godzilla   movie

Did you like the new Godzilla movie?

Adjectives are words that describe a noun (a person, place, or thing). Draw a line matching the picture with the correct adjective and noun phrase.

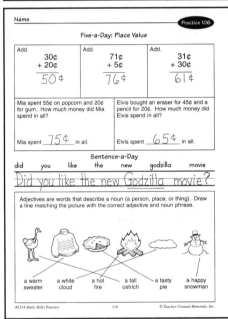

a warm sweater   a white cloud   a hot fire   a tall ostrich   a tasty pie   a happy snowman

#2514 Daily Skills Practice   110   © Teacher Created Materials, Inc.

Page 111

Five-a-Day: Place Value

Subtract.	Subtract.	Subtract.
45¢ −13¢ = **32¢**	56¢ − 5¢ = **51¢**	89¢ −80¢ = **9¢**

Helen earned 75¢ washing the car. She put 50¢ in her bank. How much money does Helen have left?

Helen has **25¢** left.

Val's grandma gave her 95¢. Val spent 50¢ on a pocket folder. How much money does she have left?

Val has **45¢** left.

Sentence-a-Day

what   does   her   feed   the   turtle

What does she feed the turtle?

Read each sentence. Circle the adjective in each sentence. Draw a line under the noun it modifies in each sentence.

1. The (happy) girl blew out the candles.
2. The (crying) man watched the movie.
3. The (sleepy) baby was in the crib.
4. The (hungry) woman ate dinner.
5. The (laughing) boy enjoyed the movie.

© Teacher Created Materials, Inc.   111   #2514 Daily Skills Practice

---

Page 112

Five-a-Day: Place Value

Subtract.	Subtract.	Subtract.
44¢ −11¢ = **33¢**	50¢ −20¢ = **30¢**	93¢ −32¢ = **61¢**

Christine cleaned the pool for 85¢. She bought a pool toy for 73¢. How much money does Christine have left?

Christine has **12** ¢ left.

Mom had 85¢ in her wallet. She spent 50¢ on a carton of juice. How much money does Mom have left?

Mom has **35** ¢ left.

Sentence-a-Day

me   and   hannah   seen   a   silver   dollar

Hannah and I saw a silver dollar.

Read each sentence. Write the missing adjective on the line.

green   purple   black   yellow   red

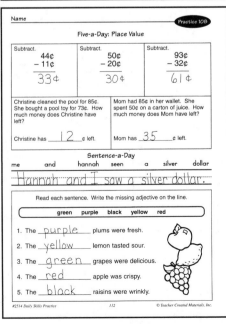

1. The **purple** plums were fresh.
2. The **yellow** lemon tasted sour.
3. The **green** grapes were delicious.
4. The **red** apple was crispy.
5. The **black** raisins were wrinkly.

#2514 Daily Skills Practice   112   © Teacher Created Materials, Inc.

Name
Practice 109

Five-a-Day: Place Value

Sari spent 29¢ on gum and 30¢ on candy. How much money did she spend in all? _59_ ¢	Rob has 25¢. He earned 10¢ more by raking leaves. How much money does Rob have? _35_ ¢	Ray has 45¢. He spent 15¢ on a toy. How much money does Ray have left? _30_ ¢
Deb has 95¢. She spends 85¢ on a toy for her cat. How much money does Deb have left? Deb has _10_ ¢ left.	Bob has 35¢. He put 20¢ into his savings account. How much money does Bob have left? Bob has _15_ ¢ left.	

Sentence-a-Day

what   you   gonna   spend   your   money   on

On what are you going to spend your money?

Read each sentence. Write the missing adjective on the line.

beautiful   woolly   prickly   buzzing   chirping

1. The _prickly_ porcupine has lots of quills.
2. The _chirping_ bird sang a song.
3. The _woolly_ sheep slept in the field.
4. The _buzzing_ bee flew in the garden.
5. The _beautiful_ butterfly was resting on a flower.

© Teacher Created Materials, Inc.   113   #2514 Daily Skills Practice

Name
Practice 110

Five-a-Day: Place Value

Add. 23 + 14 = 37	Subtract. 34 − 12 = 22	Subtract. 52 − 1 = 51
Hansel has 75 pieces of candy. He gives 35 pieces to Gretel. How many pieces of candy does Hansel have left? He has _40_ pieces of candy.	Ivan recycled 14 cans of soda and 25 bundles of newspapers. How many items did Ivan recycle in all? He recycled _39_ items.	

Sentence-a-Day

me   helped   roger   clean   up   him   room

I helped Roger clean up his room.

Look at each picture. Write the beginning and ending sound for each picture.

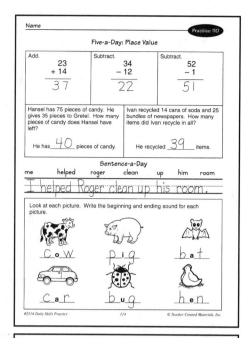

C o w   p i g   b a t

c a r   b u g   h e n

#2514 Daily Skills Practice   114   © Teacher Created Materials, Inc.

Name
Practice 111

Five-a-Day: Add and Subtract to 12

Meg has 2 bows. She buys 4 more. How many does she now have? 2 + 4 = 6	Dad has 23 ties. He gave away 11 ties. How many ties does Dad now have? 23 − 11 = 12	Leanne has 9 birds. If 3 birds fly away, how many birds are left? 9 − 3 = 6
Pao has 19 tires. Pao sells 15 of them. How many tires does Pao have left? Pao has _4_ tires left.	Sara has 17 cream pies. She sells 11 of them. How many pies does Sara now have? Sara now has _6_ pies.	

Sentence-a-Day

me   and   lee   plays   on   the   computer

Lee and I play on the computer.

Look at each picture. Write the beginning and ending sound for each picture.

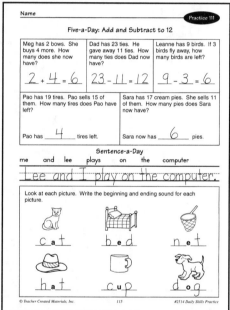

c a t   b e d   n e t

h a t   c u p   d o g

© Teacher Created Materials, Inc.   115   #2514 Daily Skills Practice

Name
Practice 112

Five-a-Day: Add and Subtract to 12

Add. 3 + 7 = 10	Add. 5 + 5 = 10	Add. 6 + 5 = 11
Add. 2 + 7 = 9 7 + 2 = 9	Add. 3 + 7 = 10 7 + 3 = 10	

Sentence-a-Day

do   charlotte   has   a   computer

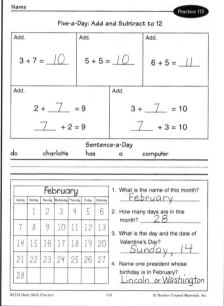

February						
Sunday	Monday	Tuesday	Wednesday	Thursday	Friday	Saturday
		1	2	3	4	5	6
7	8	9	10	11	12	13
14	15	16	17	18	19	20
21	22	23	24	25	26	27
28						

1. What is the name of this month? _February_
2. How many days are in this month? _28_
3. What is the day and the date of Valentine's Day? _Sunday, 14_
4. Name one president whose birthday is in February? _Lincoln or Washington_

#2514 Daily Skills Practice   116   © Teacher Created Materials, Inc.

Name
Practice 113

Five-a-Day: Add and Subtract to 12

Add. 4 + 8 = 12	Add. 7 + 3 = 10	Add. 5 + 6 = 11
Add. 9 + 3 = 12 3 + 9 = 12	Add. 5 + 7 = 12 7 + 5 = 12	

Sentence-a-Day

us   have   computers   at   school

We have computers at school.

Write the insects' names in alphabetical order.

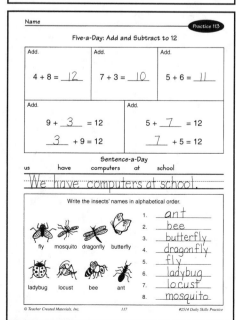

fly   mosquito   dragonfly   butterfly

ladybug   locust   bee   ant

1. _ant_
2. _bee_
3. _butterfly_
4. _dragonfly_
5. _fly_
6. _ladybug_
7. _locust_
8. _mosquito_

© Teacher Created Materials, Inc.   117   #2514 Daily Skills Practice

Name
Practice 114

Five-a-Day: Add and Subtract to 12

Add. 9 + 3 = 12	Add. 6 + 4 = 10	Add. 8 + 3 = 11
I made 1 star. My friend Mee made 8 stars. How many stars did we make in all? We made _9_ stars in all.	Dareen caught 9 butterflies. Devin caught 3 butterflies. How many butterflies did they catch? They caught _12_ butterflies in all.	

Sentence-a-Day

why   are   the   sky   black   at   night

Why is the sky black at night?

Read the scrambled sentence. Write the words in the correct order.

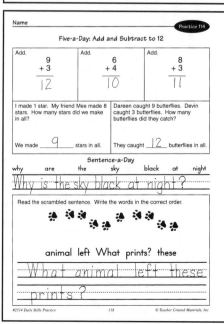

animal   left   What   prints?   these

What animal left these prints?

#2514 Daily Skills Practice   118   © Teacher Created Materials, Inc.

Page 119

Five-a-Day: Add and Subtract to 12

Add.	Add.	Add.
5 +7 = 12	4 +5 = 9	9 +2 = 11

Justin made 7 pictures using crayons and 4 pictures using chalk. How many pictures did Justin make in all?

Justin made __11__ pictures in all.

Louisa bought a dozen eggs. If 6 of the eggs broke, how many eggs does Louisa have left?

Louisa has __6__ eggs left.

Sentence-a-Day

me   helped   louisa   clean   up   the   mess

I helped Louisa clean up the mess.

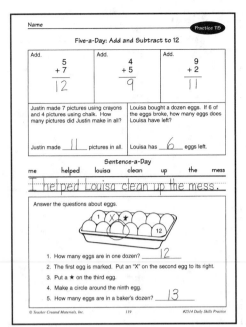

Answer the questions about eggs.

1. How many eggs are in one dozen? __12__
2. The first egg is marked. Put an "X" on the second egg to its right.
3. Put a ★ on the third egg.
4. Make a circle around the ninth egg.
5. How many eggs are in a baker's dozen? __13__

© Teacher Created Materials, Inc.   119   #2514 Daily Skills Practice

---

Page 120

Five-a-Day: Add and Subtract to 12

Add.	Add.	Add.
4 + 6 = 10	3 + 8 = 11	5 + 6 = 11
6 + 4 = 10	8 + 3 = 11	6 + 5 = 11

Use the numbers 3, 7, and 10 to make two addition problems.

3 + 7 = 10
7 + 3 = 10

Use the numbers 3, 7, and 10 to make two subtraction problems.

10 − 3 = 7
10 − 7 = 3

Sentence-a-Day

why   do   abraham   lincoln   wear   a   hat

Why does Abraham Lincoln wear a hat?

Look at each picture and its word. Write the missing vowel.
(Vowels are a, e, i, o, and u.)

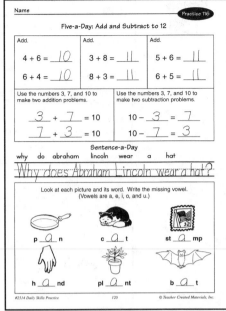

p _a_ n   c _a_ t   st _a_ mp
h _a_ nd   pl _a_ nt   b _a_ t

#2514 Daily Skills Practice   120   © Teacher Created Materials, Inc.

Page 121

Five-a-Day: Add and Subtract to 12

Add.	Add.	Add.
5 + 7 = 12	4 + 7 = 11	4 + 8 = 12
7 + 5 = 12	7 + 4 = 11	8 + 4 = 12

Use the numbers 1, 9, and 10 to make two addition problems.

9 + 1 = 10
1 + 9 = 10

Use the numbers 1, 9, and 10 to make two subtraction problems.

10 − 9 = 1
10 − 1 = 9

Sentence-a-Day

aint   his   picture   on   a   penny

Isn't his picture on a penny?

Look at each picture and its word. Write the missing vowel.
(Vowels are a, e, i, o, and u.)

r _e_ st   sl _e_ d   b _e_ nch
d _e_ sk   h _e_ n   _e_ gg

© Teacher Created Materials, Inc.   121   #2514 Daily Skills Practice

---

Page 122

Five-a-Day: Add and Subtract to 12

Add.	Add.	Add.
2 + 9 = 11	7 +5 = 12	3 + 7 = 10
9 + 2 = 11		7 + 3 = 10

Use the numbers 4, 7, and 11 to make two addition problems.

4 + 7 = 11
7 + 4 = 11

Use the numbers 4, 7, and 11 to make two subtraction problems.

11 − 7 = 4
11 − 4 = 7

Sentence-a-Day

didnt   you   watch   the   washington   parade

Didn't you watch the Washington parade?

Look at each picture and its word. Write the missing vowel.
(Vowels are a, e, i, o, and u.)

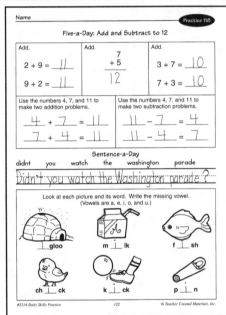

_i_ gloo   m _i_ lk   f _i_ sh
ch _i_ ck   k _i_ ck   p _i_ n

#2514 Daily Skills Practice   122   © Teacher Created Materials, Inc.

Page 123

Five-a-Day: Add and Subtract to 12

Add. Circle the doubles.	Add. Circle the doubles.	Add. Circle the doubles.
2 + 2 = 4	1 + 1 = 2	3 + 3 = 6
6 + 5 = 11	9 + 1 = 10	4 + 4 = 8

Use the numbers 5, 6, and 11 to make two addition problems.

5 + 6 = 11
6 + 5 = 11

Use the numbers 5, 6, and 11 to make two subtraction problems.

11 − 6 = 5
11 − 5 = 6

Sentence-a-Day

we   goed   to   sacramento   to   see   the   parade

We went to Sacramento to see the parade.

Look at each picture and its word. Write the missing vowel.
(Vowels are a, e, i, o, and u.)

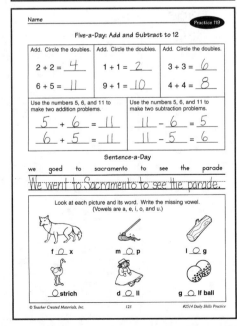

f _o_ x   m _o_ p   l _o_ g
_o_ strich   d _o_ ll   g _o_ lf ball

© Teacher Created Materials, Inc.   123   #2514 Daily Skills Practice

---

Page 124

Five-a-Day: Add and Subtract to 14

Circle the answer.	Circle the answer.	Circle the answer.
Pete has 4 rocks. He finds 5 more. How many does he have in all?	If 7 mice were sitting and 4 mice ran away how many mice were left?	If 11 horses were eating and 3 horses stopped eating how many horses were eating?
(9) 17	9 (3)	12 (8)

Use the numbers 3, 9, and 12 to make two addition problems.

3 + 9 = 12
9 + 3 = 12

Use the numbers 3, 9, and 12 to make two subtraction problems.

12 − 9 = 3
12 − 3 = 9

Sentence-a-Day

cant   you   run   any   faster

Can't you run any faster?

Look at each picture and its word. Write the missing vowel.
(Vowels are a, e, i, o, and u.)

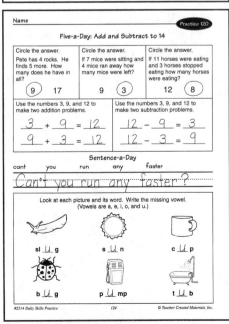

sl _u_ g   s _u_ n   c _u_ p
b _u_ g   p _u_ mp   t _u_ b

#2514 Daily Skills Practice   124   © Teacher Created Materials, Inc.

Page 125

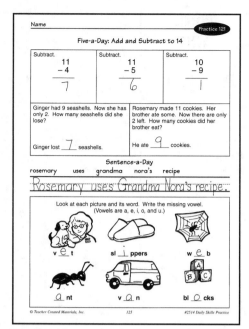

Practice 121

Five-a-Day: Add and Subtract to 14

Subtract. $\begin{array}{r} 11 \\ -\ 4 \\ \hline 7 \end{array}$	Subtract. $\begin{array}{r} 11 \\ -\ 5 \\ \hline 6 \end{array}$	Subtract. $\begin{array}{r} 10 \\ -\ 9 \\ \hline 1 \end{array}$
Ginger had 9 seashells. Now she has only 2. How many seashells did she lose? Ginger lost 7 seashells.	Rosemary made 11 cookies. Her brother ate some. Now there are only 2 left. How many cookies did her brother eat? He ate 9 cookies.	

Sentence-a-Day

rosemary uses grandma nora's recipe

Rosemary uses Grandma Nora's recipe.

Look at each picture and its word. Write the missing vowel.
(Vowels are a, e, i, o, and u.)

v e t   sl i ppers   w e b

a nt   v a n   bl o cks

© Teacher Created Materials, Inc.   125   #2514 Daily Skills Practice

---

Page 126

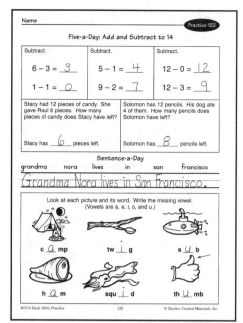

Practice 122

Five-a-Day: Add and Subtract to 14

Subtract. $6 - 3 = 3$ $1 - 1 = 0$	Subtract. $5 - 1 = 4$ $9 - 2 = 7$	Subtract. $12 - 0 = 12$ $12 - 3 = 9$
Stacy had 12 pieces of candy. She gave Raul 6 pieces. How many pieces of candy does Stacy have left? Stacy has 6 pieces left.	Solomon has 12 pencils. His dog ate 4 of them. How many pencils does Solomon have left? Solomon has 8 pencils left.	

Sentence-a-Day

grandma nora lives in san francisco

Grandma Nora lives in San Francisco.

Look at each picture and its word. Write the missing vowel.
(Vowels are a, e, i, o, and u.)

c a mp   tw i g   s u b

h a m   squ i d   th u mb

#2514 Daily Skills Practice   126   © Teacher Created Materials, Inc.

Page 127

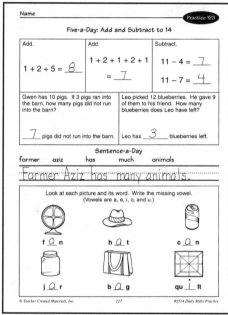

Practice 123

Five-a-Day: Add and Subtract to 14

Add. $1 + 2 + 5 = 8$	Add. $1 + 2 + 1 + 2 + 1$ $= 7$	Subtract. $11 - 4 = 7$ $11 - 7 = 4$
Gwen has 10 pigs. If 3 pigs ran into the barn, how many pigs did not run into the barn? 7 pigs did not run into the barn.	Leo picked 12 blueberries. He gave 9 of them to his friend. How many blueberries does Leo have left? Leo has 3 blueberries left.	

Sentence-a-Day

farmer aziz has much animals

Farmer Aziz has many animals.

Look at each picture and its word. Write the missing vowel.
(Vowels are a, e, i, o, and u.)

f a n   h a t   c a n

j a r   b a g   qu i lt

© Teacher Created Materials, Inc.   127   #2514 Daily Skills Practice

---

Page 128

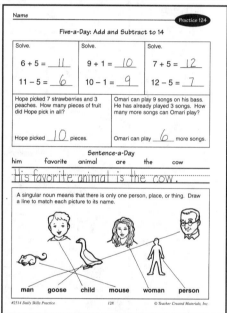

Practice 124

Five-a-Day: Add and Subtract to 14

Solve. $6 + 5 = 11$ $11 - 5 = 6$	Solve. $9 + 1 = 10$ $10 - 1 = 9$	Solve. $7 + 5 = 12$ $12 - 5 = 7$
Hope picked 7 strawberries and 3 peaches. How many pieces of fruit did Hope pick in all? Hope picked 10 pieces.	Omari can play 9 songs on his bass. He has already played 3 songs. How many more songs can Omari play? Omari can play 6 more songs.	

Sentence-a-Day

him favorite animal are the cow

His favorite animal is the cow.

A singular noun means that there is only one person, place, or thing. Draw a line to match each picture to its name.

man   goose   child   mouse   woman   person

#2514 Daily Skills Practice   128   © Teacher Created Materials, Inc.

Page 129

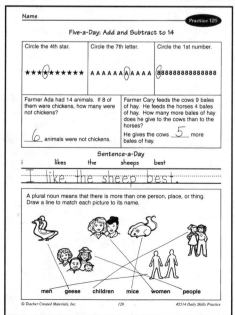

Practice 125

Five-a-Day: Add and Subtract to 14

Circle the 4th star. ★★★⊛★★★★★★	Circle the 7th letter. AAAAAAⒶAAAA	Circle the 1st number. ⑧8888888888888
Farmer Ada had 14 animals. If 8 of them were chickens, how many were not chickens? 6 animals were not chickens.	Farmer Cary feeds the cows 9 bales of hay. He feeds the horses 4 bales of hay. How many more bales of hay does he give to the cows than to the horses? He gives the cows 5 more bales of hay.	

Sentence-a-Day

i likes the sheeps best

I like the sheep best.

A plural noun means that there is more than one person, place, or thing. Draw a line to match each picture to its name.

men   geese   children   mice   women   people

© Teacher Created Materials, Inc.   129   #2514 Daily Skills Practice

---

Page 130

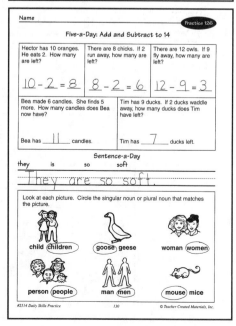

Practice 126

Five-a-Day: Add and Subtract to 14

Hector has 10 oranges. He eats 2. How many are left? $10 - 2 = 8$	There are 8 chicks. If 2 run away, how many are left? $8 - 2 = 6$	There are 12 owls. If 9 fly away, how many are left? $12 - 9 = 3$
Bea made 6 candles. She finds 5 more. How many candles does Bea now have? Bea has 11 candles.	Tim has 9 ducks. If 2 ducks waddle away, how many ducks does Tim have left? Tim has 7 ducks left.	

Sentence-a-Day

they is so soft

They are so soft.

Look at each picture. Circle the singular noun or plural noun that matches the picture.

child (children)   goose (geese)   woman (women)

person (people)   man (men)   (mouse) mice

#2514 Daily Skills Practice   130   © Teacher Created Materials, Inc.

Page 131

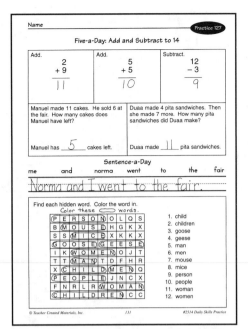

Page 132

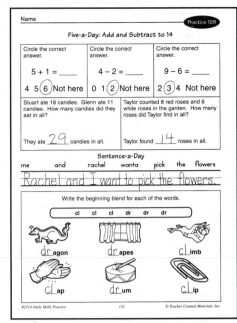

Page 133

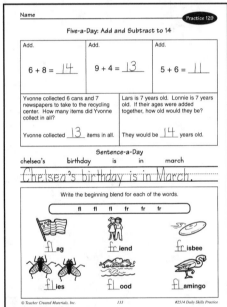

Page 134

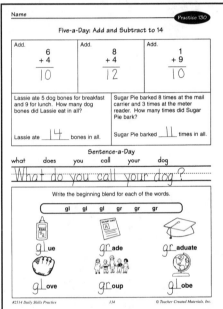

Page 135

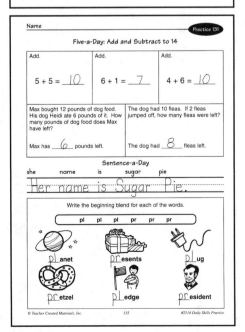

Page 136

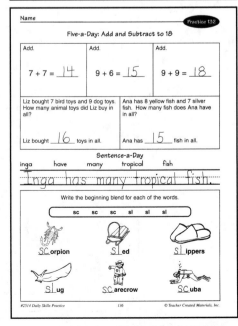

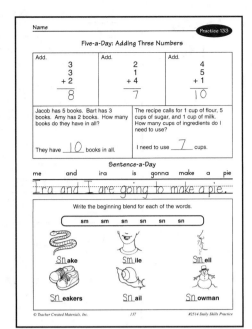

Page 137 — Practice 133 — Five-a-Day: Adding Three Numbers

Add.	Add.	Add.
3	2	4
3	1	5
+ 2	+ 4	+ 1
8	7	10

Jacob has 5 books. Bart has 3 books. Amy has 2 books. How many books do they have in all?

They have 10 books in all.

The recipe calls for 1 cup of flour, 5 cups of sugar, and 1 cup of milk. How many cups of ingredients do I need to use?

I need to use 7 cups.

Sentence-a-Day

me   and   ira   is   gonna   make   a   pie

Ira and I are going to make a pie.

Write the beginning blend for each of the words.

sm   sm   sn   sn   sn   sn

Sn ake   Sm ile   Sm ell
Sn eakers   Sn ail   Sn owman

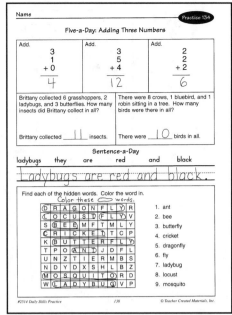

Page 138 — Practice 134 — Five-a-Day: Adding Three Numbers

Add.	Add.	Add.
3	3	2
1	5	2
+ 0	+ 4	+ 2
4	12	6

Brittany collected 6 grasshoppers, 2 ladybugs, and 3 butterflies. How many insects did Brittany collect in all?

Brittany collected 11 insects.

There were 8 crows, 1 bluebird, and 1 robin sitting in a tree. How many birds were there in all?

There were 10 birds in all.

Sentence-a-Day

ladybugs   they   are   red   and   black

Ladybugs are red and black.

Find each of the hidden words. Color the word in. Color these words.

1. ant
2. bee
3. butterfly
4. cricket
5. dragonfly
6. fly
7. ladybug
8. locust
9. mosquito

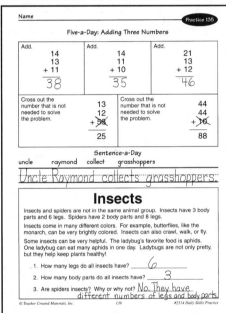

Page 139 — Practice 135 — Five-a-Day: Adding Three Numbers

Add.	Add.	Add.
14	14	21
13	11	13
+ 11	+ 10	+ 12
38	35	46

Cross out the number that is not needed to solve the problem.
13
12
+ 58 ~~crossed out~~
25

Cross out the number that is not needed to solve the problem.
44
44
+ 16 ~~crossed out~~
88

Sentence-a-Day

uncle   raymond   collect   grasshoppers

Uncle Raymond collects grasshoppers.

Insects

Insects and spiders are not in the same animal group. Insects have 3 body parts and 6 legs. Spiders have 2 body parts and 8 legs.

Insects come in many different colors. For example, butterflies, like the monarch, can be very brightly colored. Insects can also crawl, walk, or fly.

Some insects can be very helpful. The ladybug's favorite food is aphids. One ladybug can eat many aphids in one day. Ladybugs are not only pretty, but they help keep plants healthy!

1. How many legs do all insects have? 6
2. How many body parts do all insects have? 3
3. Are spiders insects? Why or why not? No. They have different numbers of legs and body parts.

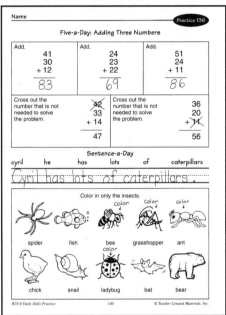

Page 140 — Practice 136 — Five-a-Day: Adding Three Numbers

Add.	Add.	Add.
41	24	51
30	23	24
+ 12	+ 22	+ 11
83	69	86

Cross out the number that is not needed to solve the problem.
~~42~~
33
+ 14
47

Cross out the number that is not needed to solve the problem.
36
20
+ ~~11~~
56

Sentence-a-Day

cyril   he   has   lots   of   caterpillars

Cyril has lots of caterpillars.

Color in only the insects.

color   color   color
spider   fish   bee   grasshopper   ant
color
chick   snail   ladybug   bat   bear

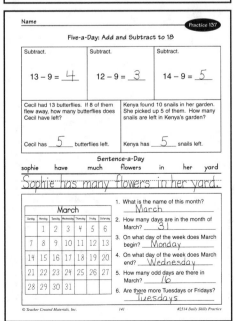

Page 141 — Practice 137 — Five-a-Day: Add and Subtract to 18

Subtract.	Subtract.	Subtract.
$13 - 9 = 4$	$12 - 9 = 3$	$14 - 9 = 5$

Cecil had 13 butterflies. If 8 of them flew away, how many butterflies does Cecil have left?

Cecil has 5 butterflies left.

Kenya found 10 snails in her garden. She picked up 5 of them. How many snails are left in Kenya's garden?

Kenya has 5 snails left.

Sentence-a-Day

sophie   have   much   flowers   in   her   yard

Sophie has many flowers in her yard.

March

Sunday	Monday	Tuesday	Wednesday	Thursday	Friday	Saturday
		1	2	3	4	5
6	7	8	9	10	11	12
13	14	15	16	17	18	19
20	21	22	23	24	25	26
27	28	29	30	31		

1. What is the name of this month? March
2. How many days are in the month of March? 31
3. On what day of the week does March begin? Monday
4. On what day of the week does March end? Wednesday
5. How many odd days are there in March? 16
6. Are there more Tuesdays or Fridays? Tuesdays

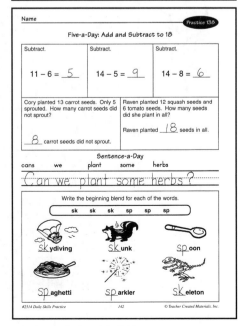

Page 142 — Practice 138 — Five-a-Day: Add and Subtract to 18

Subtract.	Subtract.	Subtract.
$11 - 6 = 5$	$14 - 5 = 9$	$14 - 8 = 6$

Cory planted 13 carrot seeds. Only 5 sprouted. How many carrot seeds did not sprout?

8 carrot seeds did not sprout.

Raven planted 12 squash seeds and 6 tomato seeds. How many seeds did she plant in all?

Raven planted 18 seeds in all.

Sentence-a-Day

cans   we   plant   some   herbs

Can we plant some herbs?

Write the beginning blend for each of the words.

sk   sk   sk   sp   sp   sp

Sk ydiving   Sk unk   Sp oon
Sp aghetti   Sp arkler   Sk eleton

Page 143

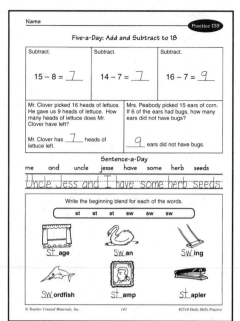

Name _____

Practice 139

Five-a-Day: Add and Subtract to 18

Subtract.	Subtract.	Subtract.
15 − 8 = 7	14 − 7 = 7	16 − 7 = 9

Mr. Clover picked 16 heads of lettuce. He gave us 9 heads of lettuce. How many heads of lettuce does Mr. Clover have left?

Mr. Clover has 7 heads of lettuce left.

Mrs. Peabody picked 15 ears of corn. If 6 of the ears had bugs, how many ears did not have bugs?

9 ears did not have bugs.

Sentence-a-Day

me and uncle jesse have some herb seeds

Uncle Jess and I have some herb seeds.

Write the beginning blend for each of the words.

st   st   st   sw   sw   sw

st age   sw an   sw ing

sw ordfish   st amp   st apler

© Teacher Created Materials, Inc.   143   #2514 Daily Skills Practice

---

Page 144

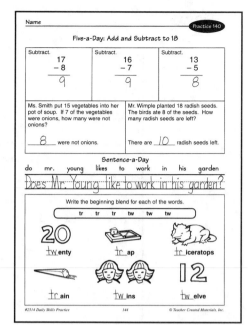

Name _____

Practice 140

Five-a-Day: Add and Subtract to 18

Subtract.	Subtract.	Subtract.
17 − 8 = 9	16 − 7 = 9	13 − 5 = 8

Ms. Smith put 15 vegetables into her pot of soup. If 7 of the vegetables were onions, how many were not onions?

8 were not onions.

Mr. Wimple planted 18 radish seeds. The birds ate 8 of the seeds. How many radish seeds are left?

There are 10 radish seeds left.

Sentence-a-Day

do mr. young likes to work in his garden

Does Mr. Young like to work in his garden?

Write the beginning blend for each of the words.

tr   tr   tr   tw   tw   tw

tw enty   tr ap   tr iceratops

tr ain   tw ins   tw elve

#2514 Daily Skills Practice   144   © Teacher Created Materials, Inc.

Page 145

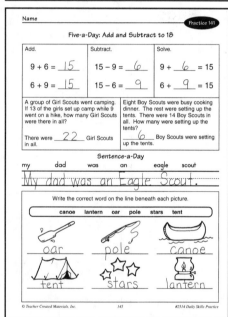

Name _____

Practice 141

Five-a-Day: Add and Subtract to 18

Add.	Subtract.	Solve.
9 + 6 = 15	15 − 9 = 6	9 + 6 = 15
6 + 9 = 15	15 − 6 = 9	6 + 9 = 15

A group of Girl Scouts went camping. If 13 of the girls set up camp while 9 went on a hike, how many Girl Scouts were there in all?

There were 22 Girl Scouts in all.

Eight Boy Scouts were busy cooking dinner. The rest were setting up the tents. There were 14 Boy Scouts in all. How many were setting up the tents?

6 Boy Scouts were setting up the tents.

Sentence-a-Day

my dad was an eagle scout

My dad was an Eagle Scout.

Write the correct word on the line beneath each picture.

canoe   lantern   oar   pole   stars   tent

oar   pole   canoe

tent   stars   lantern

© Teacher Created Materials, Inc.   145   #2514 Daily Skills Practice

---

Page 146

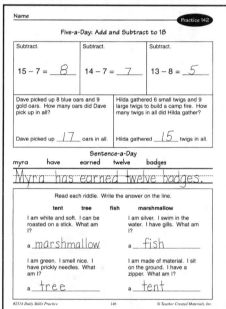

Name _____

Practice 142

Five-a-Day: Add and Subtract to 18

Subtract.	Subtract.	Subtract.
15 − 7 = 8	14 − 7 = 7	13 − 8 = 5

Dave picked up 8 blue oars and 9 gold oars. How many oars did Dave pick up in all?

Dave picked up 17 oars in all.

Hilda gathered 6 small twigs and 9 large twigs to build a camp fire. How many twigs in all did Hilda gather?

Hilda gathered 15 twigs in all.

Sentence-a-Day

myra have earned twelve badges

Myra has earned twelve badges.

Read each riddle. Write the answer on the line.

tent   tree   fish   marshmallow

I am white and soft. I can be roasted on a stick. What am I?

a marshmallow

I am silver. I swim in the water. I have gills. What am I?

a fish

I am green. I smell nice. I have prickly needles. What am I?

a tree

I am made of material. I sit on the ground. I have a zipper. What am I?

a tent

#2514 Daily Skills Practice   146   © Teacher Created Materials, Inc.

Page 147

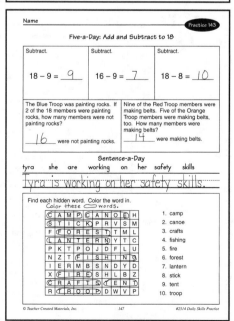

Name _____

Practice 143

Five-a-Day: Add and Subtract to 18

Subtract.	Subtract.	Subtract.
18 − 9 = 9	16 − 9 = 7	18 − 8 = 10

The Blue Troop was painting rocks. If 2 of the 18 members were painting rocks, how many members were not painting rocks?

16 were not painting rocks.

Nine of the Red Troop members were making belts. Five of the Orange Troop members were making belts, too. How many members were making belts?

14 were making belts.

Sentence-a-Day

tyra she are working on her safety skills

Tyra is working on her safety skills.

Find each hidden word. Color the word in.
Color these ⬭ words.

C	A	M	P	C	A	N	O	E	H
S	T	I	C	K	P	R	V	S	M
F	O	R	E	S	T	T	M	L	L
L	A	N	T	E	R	N	Y	T	C
P	K	T	P	O	J	D	F	L	U
N	Z	T	F	I	S	H	I	N	G
I	E	R	M	B	S	N	D	Y	D
X	F	I	R	E	S	H	L	B	Z
C	R	A	F	T	S	T	E	N	T
R	T	R	O	O	D	D	W	V	P

1. camp
2. canoe
3. crafts
4. fishing
5. fire
6. forest
7. lantern
8. stick
9. tent
10. troop

© Teacher Created Materials, Inc.   147   #2514 Daily Skills Practice

---

Page 148

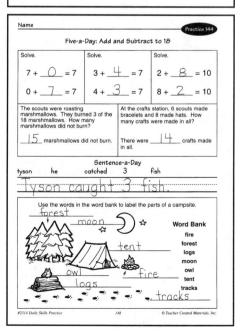

Name _____

Practice 144

Five-a-Day: Add and Subtract to 18

Solve.	Solve.	Solve.
7 + 0 = 7	3 + 4 = 7	2 + 8 = 10
0 + 7 = 7	4 + 3 = 7	8 + 2 = 10

The scouts were roasting marshmallows. They burned 3 of the 18 marshmallows. How many marshmallows did not burn?

15 marshmallows did not burn.

At the crafts station, 6 scouts made bracelets and 8 made hats. How many crafts were made in all?

There were 14 crafts made in all.

Sentence-a-Day

tyson he catched 3 fish

Tyson caught 3 fish.

Use the words in the word bank to label the parts of a campsite.

forest   moon   tent   owl   logs   fire   tracks

Word Bank
fire
forest
logs
moon
owl
tent
tracks

#2514 Daily Skills Practice   148   © Teacher Created Materials, Inc.

Page 149

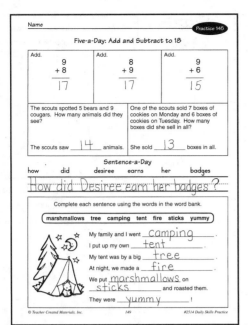

Five-a-Day: Add and Subtract to 18

Add.	Add.	Add.
9 + 8 = 17	8 + 9 = 17	9 + 6 = 15

The scouts spotted 5 bears and 9 cougars. How many animals did they see?

The scouts saw __14__ animals.

One of the scouts sold 7 boxes of cookies on Monday and 6 boxes of cookies on Tuesday. How many boxes did she sell in all?

She sold __13__ boxes in all.

Sentence-a-Day

how   did   desiree   earns   her   badges

How did Desiree earn her badges?

Complete each sentence using the words in the word bank.

marshmallows   tree   camping   tent   fire   sticks   yummy

My family and I went __camping__.
I put up my own __tent__.
My tent was by a big __tree__.
At night, we made a __fire__.
We put __marshmallows__ on __sticks__ and roasted them.
They were __yummy__!

© Teacher Created Materials, Inc.   149   #2514 Daily Skills Practice

Page 150

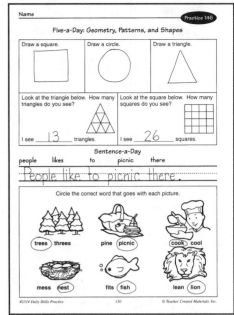

Five-a-Day: Geometry, Patterns, and Shapes

Draw a square.	Draw a circle.	Draw a triangle.

Look at the triangle below. How many triangles do you see?	Look at the square below. How many squares do you see?
I see __13__ triangles.	I see __26__ squares.

Sentence-a-Day

people   likes   to   picnic   there

People like to picnic there.

Circle the correct word that goes with each picture.

trees / (threes)   pine / (picnic)   (cook) / cool

mess / (nest)   fits / (fish)   lean / (lion)

#2514 Daily Skills Practice   150   © Teacher Created Materials, Inc.

Page 151

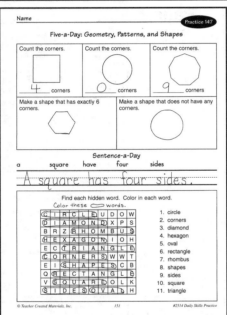

Five-a-Day: Geometry, Patterns, and Shapes

Count the corners.	Count the corners.	Count the corners.
__4__ corners	_____ corners	__9__ corners

Make a shape that has exactly 6 corners.	Make a shape that does not have any corners.

Sentence-a-Day

a   square   have   four   sides

A square has four sides.

Find each hidden word. Color in each word.
Color these words.

1. circle
2. corners
3. diamond
4. hexagon
5. oval
6. rectangle
7. rhombus
8. shapes
9. sides
10. square
11. triangle

© Teacher Created Materials, Inc.   151   #2514 Daily Skills Practice

Page 152

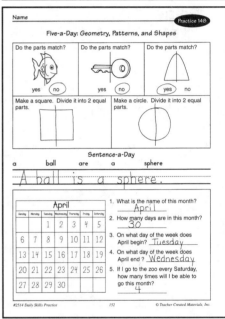

Five-a-Day: Geometry, Patterns, and Shapes

Do the parts match?	Do the parts match?	Do the parts match?
yes / (no)	yes / (no)	(yes) / no

Make a square. Divide it into 2 equal parts.	Make a circle. Divide it into 2 equal parts.

Sentence-a-Day

a   ball   are   a   sphere

A ball is a sphere.

April						
Sunday	Monday	Tuesday	Wednesday	Thursday	Friday	Saturday
		1	2	3	4	5
6	7	8	9	10	11	12
13	14	15	16	17	18	19
20	21	22	23	24	25	26
27	28	29	30			

1. What is the name of this month? __April__
2. How many days are in this month? __30__
3. On what day of the week does April begin? __Tuesday__
4. On what day of the week does April end? __Wednesday__
5. If I go to the zoo every Saturday, how many times will I be able to go this month? __4__

#2514 Daily Skills Practice   152   © Teacher Created Materials, Inc.

Page 153

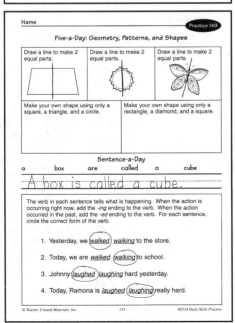

Five-a-Day: Geometry, Patterns, and Shapes

Draw a line to make 2 equal parts.	Draw a line to make 2 equal parts.	Draw a line to make 2 equal parts.

Make your own shape using only a square, a triangle, and a circle.	Make your own shape using only a rectangle, a diamond, and a square.

Sentence-a-Day

a   box   are   called   a   cube

A box is called a cube.

The verb in each sentence tells what is happening. When the action is occurring right now, add the -ing ending to the verb. When the action occurred in the past, add the -ed ending to the verb. For each sentence, circle the correct form of the verb.

1. Yesterday, we (walked) / walking to the store.
2. Today, we are walked / (walking) to school.
3. Johnny (laughed) / laughing hard yesterday.
4. Today, Ramona is laughed / (laughing) really hard.

© Teacher Created Materials, Inc.   153   #2514 Daily Skills Practice

Page 154

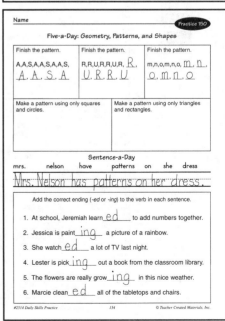

Five-a-Day: Geometry, Patterns, and Shapes

Finish the pattern.	Finish the pattern.	Finish the pattern.
A,A,S,A,A,S,A,A,S, __A,A,S,A__	R,R,U,R,R,U,R, __R,U,R,R,U__	m,n,o,m,n,o, __m,n,o,m,n,o__

Make a pattern using only squares and circles.	Make a pattern using only triangles and rectangles.

Sentence-a-Day

mrs.   nelson   have   patterns   on   she   dress

Mrs. Nelson has patterns on her dress.

Add the correct ending (-ed or -ing) to the verb in each sentence.

1. At school, Jeremiah learn__ed__ to add numbers together.
2. Jessica is paint__ing__ a picture of a rainbow.
3. She watch__ed__ a lot of TV last night.
4. Lester is pick__ing__ out a book from the classroom library.
5. The flowers are really grow__ing__ in this nice weather.
6. Marcie clean__ed__ all of the tabletops and chairs.

#2514 Daily Skills Practice   154   © Teacher Created Materials, Inc.

Page 155

Five-a-Day: Geometry, Patterns, and Shapes

Finish the pattern.	Finish the pattern.	Finish the pattern.
S,T,U,S,T,U,S, _T_, _U_,_S_,_T_,_U_	X,Y,Z,X,Y, _Z_, _X_, _Y_,_Z_,_X_,_Y_	3,5,7,3,5,7,3, _5_, _7_,_3_,_5_,_7_
Make a pattern using 3 different numbers.	Make a pattern using 3 different letters.	

Sentence-a-Day

me   can   see   the   stars   and   stripes   pattern

I can see the stars and stripes pattern.

Add the correct ending (-ed or -ing) to the verb in each sentence.

1. Pablo is clean_ing_ his bedroom.
2. Henry scrubb_ed_ all of the pots and pans.
3. Mrs. Smith is driv_ing_ her car.
4. Ralph bark_ed_ all night at the cat.
5. Shirley pack_ed_ her suitcase.

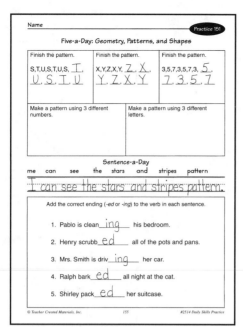

Page 156

Five-a-Day: Geometry, Patterns, and Shapes

Count the corners.	Count the corners.	Count the corners.
_3_ corners	_0_ corners	_5_ corners
Circle the shape that has 6 corners.		Circle the shape that has 3 corners.

Sentence-a-Day

lets   count   all   the   stars

Let's count all the stars.

Add the correct ending (-ed or -ing) to the verb in each sentence.

1. The custodian is wash_ing_ all of the classroom windows.
2. Brent cook_ed_ spaghetti for dinner last night.
3. Holly collect_ed_ dolls when she was younger.
4. Timothy is play_ing_ with his toys.
5. Who is watch_ing_ the children?
6. I am call_ing_ my friend in Texas.

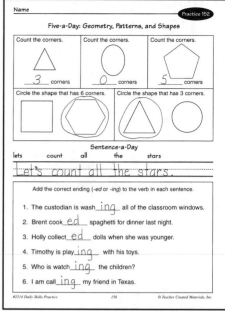

Page 157

Five-a-Day: Geometry, Patterns, and Shapes

How many square units?	How many square units?	How many square units?
_2_ square units.	_4_ square units.	_4_ square units.
Make a shape with 6 squares.	Make a shape with 9 squares.	

Sentence-a-Day

we   is   gonna   make   box   kites

We are going to make box kites.

Add the correct ending (-ed or -ing) to the verb in each sentence.

1. Mary is typ_ing_ on the computer.
2. Is Garth rak_ing_ the leaves?
3. Sylvester chang_ed_ the channel.
4. George play_ed_ soccer with Larry last night.
5. Floyd repair_ed_ the van.
6. Mary Lou is wax_ing_ the truck.

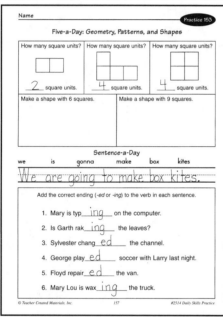

Page 158

Five-a-Day: Geometry, Patterns, and Shapes

Circle the shape that shows equal parts.	Circle the shape that shows equal parts.	Circle the shape that shows equal parts.
Circle the shape that shows 3 equal parts.		Circle the shape that shows 4 equal parts.

Sentence-a-Day

please   count   all   of   the   triangles

Please count all of the triangles.

Read the scrambled sentence. Write the words in the correct order.

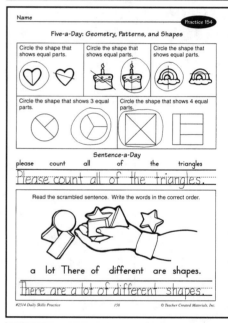

a   lot   There   of   different   are   shapes.

There are a lot of different shapes.

Page 159

Five-a-Day: Add and Subtract to 18

Add.	Subtract.	Add.
8 + 9 _17_	13 − 6 _7_	7 + 4 _11_
Jamal had 5 rolling pins. If 3 of them rolled off of the table, how many are left on the table? There are _2_ rolling pins left.	Alvin found 16 cardboard boxes. He flattened 8 of them. How many of them had not been flattened? _8_ boxes had not been flattened.	

Sentence-a-Day

lets   play   the   shapes   game

Let's play the shapes game.

Read the scrambled words. Write the sentence correctly on the lines.

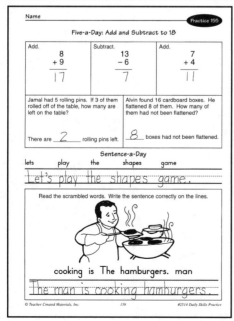

cooking   is   The   hamburgers.   man

The man is cooking hamburgers.

Page 160

Five-a-Day: Geometry, Patterns, and Shapes

Color in the shape to show ½.	Color in the shape to show ½.	Color in the shape to show ½.
Circle the shape that shows ½.		Circle the shape that shows ½.

Sentence-a-Day

mr   menio   cutted   the   cake   in   half

Mr. Menio cut the cake in half.

Rhyming words have the same ending sounds.
For example, cat and hat are two words that rhyme.
Draw a line to match each of the two pictures that rhyme.

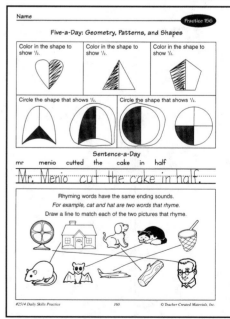

Page 161

Page 162

Page 163

Page 164

Page 165

Page 166

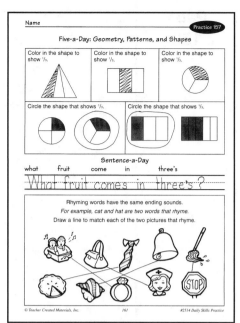

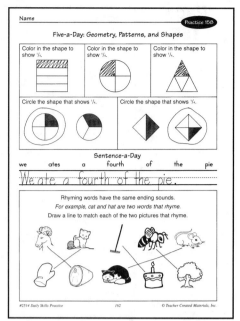

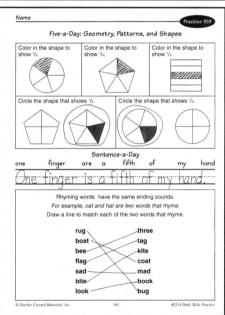

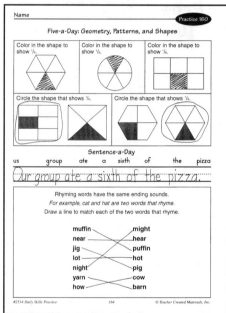

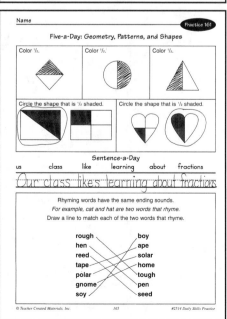

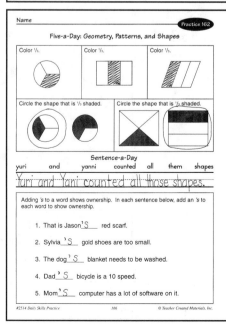

Page 167

Practice 163

Five-a-Day: Geometry, Patterns, and Shapes

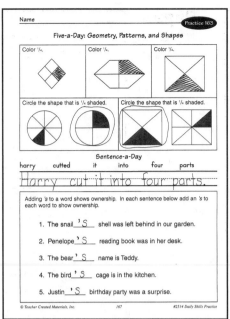

Color ¼.   Color ¼.   Color ¼.

Circle the shape that is ¼ shaded.   Circle the shape that is ¼ shaded.

Sentence-a-Day

harry   cutted   it   into   four   parts

Harry cut it into four parts.

Adding 's to a word shows ownership. In each sentence below add an 's to each word to show ownership.

1. The snail **'s** shell was left behind in our garden.

2. Penelope **'s** reading book was in her desk.

3. The bear **'s** name is Teddy.

4. The bird **'s** cage is in the kitchen.

5. Justin **'s** birthday party was a surprise.

© Teacher Created Materials, Inc.   167   #2514 Daily Skills Practice

---

Page 168

Practice 164

Five-a-Day: Geometry, Patterns, and Shapes

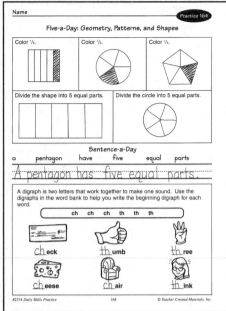

Color ⅕.   Color ⅕.   Color ⅕.

Divide the shape into 5 equal parts.   Divide the circle into 5 equal parts.

Sentence-a-Day

a   pentagon   have   five   equal   parts

A pentagon has five equal parts.

A digraph is two letters that work together to make one sound. Use the digraphs in the word bank to help you write the beginning digraph for each word.

ch   ch   ch   th   th   th

ch eck   **th** umb   **th** ree

ch eese   **ch** air   **th** ink

#2514 Daily Skills Practice   168   © Teacher Created Materials, Inc.

Page 169

Practice 165

Five-a-Day: Add and Subtract to 18

Add.
$$\begin{array}{r} 9 \\ +9 \\ \hline 18 \end{array}$$

Subtract.
$$\begin{array}{r} 16 \\ -3 \\ \hline 13 \end{array}$$

Add.
$$\begin{array}{r} 9 \\ +8 \\ \hline 17 \end{array}$$

Circle the correct answer.
King Joseph had 9 kingdoms. He sold all of them. How many kingdoms does he have left?

18 kingdoms   (0 kingdoms)

Circle the correct answer.
Mrs. Jones had 9 workers in her store. She hired 7 more. How many workers does she now have?

2 workers   (16 workers)

Sentence-a-Day

bud   and   lou   seen   a   movie

Bud and Lou saw a movie.

A digraph is two letters that work together to make one sound. Use the digraphs in the word bank to help you write the beginning digraph for each word.

sh   sh   sh   wh   wh   wh

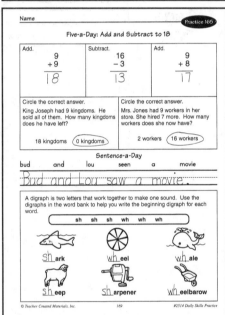

sh ark   **wh** eel   **wh** ale

sh eep   **sh** arpener   **wh** eelbarow

© Teacher Created Materials, Inc.   169   #2514 Daily Skills Practice

---

Page 170

Practice 166

Five-a-Day: Geometry, Patterns, and Shapes

What part is shaded?   What part is shaded?   What part is shaded?

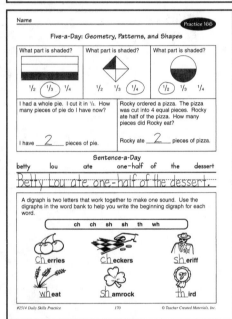

½   (⅓)   ¼   ½   ⅓   (¼)   (½)   ⅓   ¼

I had a whole pie. I cut it in ½. How many pieces of pie do I have now?

I have **2** pieces of pie.

Rocky ordered a pizza. The pizza was cut into 4 equal pieces. Rocky ate half of the pizza. How many pieces did Rocky eat?

Rocky ate **2** pieces of pizza.

Sentence-a-Day

betty   lou   ate   one-half   of   the   dessert

Betty Lou ate one-half of the dessert.

A digraph is two letters that work together to make one sound. Use the digraphs in the word bank to help you write the beginning digraph for each word.

ch   ch   sh   sh   th   wh

ch erries   **ch** eckers   **sh** eriff

wh eat   **sh** amrock   **th** ird

#2514 Daily Skills Practice   170   © Teacher Created Materials, Inc.

Page 171

Practice 167

Five-a-Day: Geometry, Patterns, and Shapes

What part is shaded?   What part is shaded?   What part is shaded?

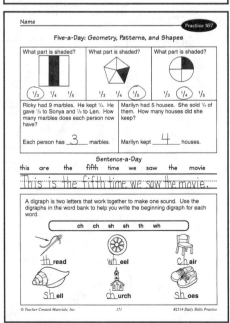

(⅓)   ¼   ⅕   ⅓   ¼   (⅕)   ⅓   (¼)   ⅕

Ricky had 9 marbles. He kept ⅓. He gave ⅓ to Sonya and ⅓ to Len. How many marbles does each person now have?

Each person has **3** marbles.

Marilyn had 5 houses. She sold ⅕ of them. How many houses did she keep?

Marilyn kept **4** houses.

Sentence-a-Day

this   are   the   fifth   time   we   saw   the   movie

This is the fifth time we saw the movie.

A digraph is two letters that work together to make one sound. Use the digraphs in the word bank to help you write the beginning digraph for each word.

ch   ch   sh   sh   th   wh

th read   **wh** eel   **ch** air

sh ell   **ch** urch   **sh** oes

© Teacher Created Materials, Inc.   171   #2514 Daily Skills Practice

---

Page 172

Practice 168

Five-a-Day: Geometry, Patterns, and Shapes

What part is shaded?   What part is shaded?   What part is shaded?

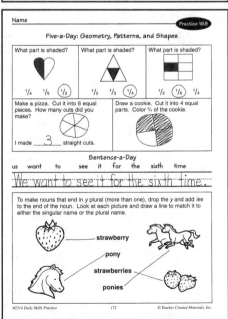

¼   ⅕   (½)   ½   ⅓   (¼)   ½   (⅙)   ¼

Make a pizza. Cut it into 6 pieces. How many cuts did you make?

I made **3** straight cuts.

Draw a cookie. Cut it into 4 equal parts. Color ¾ of the cookie.

Sentence-a-Day

us   want   to   see   it   for   the   sixth   time

We want to see it for the sixth time.

To make nouns that end in y plural (more than one), drop the y and add *ies* to the end of the noun. Look at each picture and draw a line to match it to either the singular name or the plural name.

strawberry

pony

strawberries

ponies

#2514 Daily Skills Practice   172   © Teacher Created Materials, Inc.

Page 173

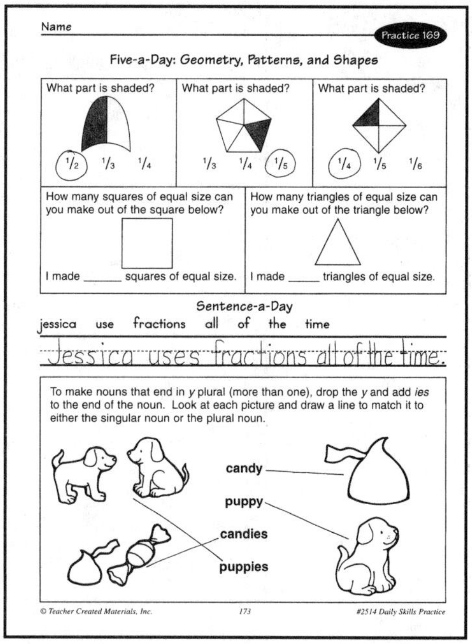

Name Practice 169

Five-a-Day: Geometry, Patterns, and Shapes

What part is shaded?	What part is shaded?	What part is shaded?
1/2 1/3 1/4	1/3 1/4 1/5	1/4 1/5 1/6

How many squares of equal size can you make out of the square below?	How many triangles of equal size can you make out of the triangle below?
I made ______ squares of equal size.	I made ______ triangles of equal size.

Sentence-a-Day

jessica use fractions all of the time

Jessica uses fractions all of the time.

To make nouns that end in *y* plural (more than one), drop the *y* and add *ies* to the end of the noun. Look at each picture and draw a line to match it to either the singular noun or the plural noun.

candy

puppy

candies

puppies

© Teacher Created Materials, Inc. 173 #2514 Daily Skills Practice

Page 174

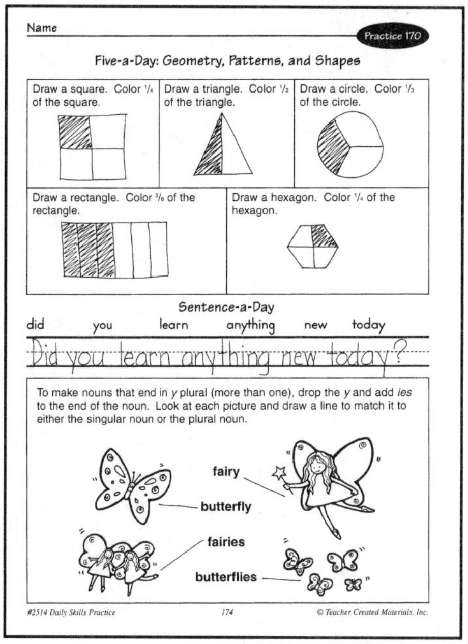

Name Practice 170

Five-a-Day: Geometry, Patterns, and Shapes

Draw a square. Color 1/4 of the square.	Draw a triangle. Color 1/2 of the triangle.	Draw a circle. Color 1/3 of the circle.

Draw a rectangle. Color 3/6 of the rectangle.	Draw a hexagon. Color 1/4 of the hexagon.

Sentence-a-Day

did you learn anything new today

Did you learn anything new today?

To make nouns that end in *y* plural (more than one), drop the *y* and add *ies* to the end of the noun. Look at each picture and draw a line to match it to either the singular noun or the plural noun.

fairy

butterfly

fairies

butterflies

#2514 Daily Skills Practice 174 © Teacher Created Materials, Inc.

Page 175

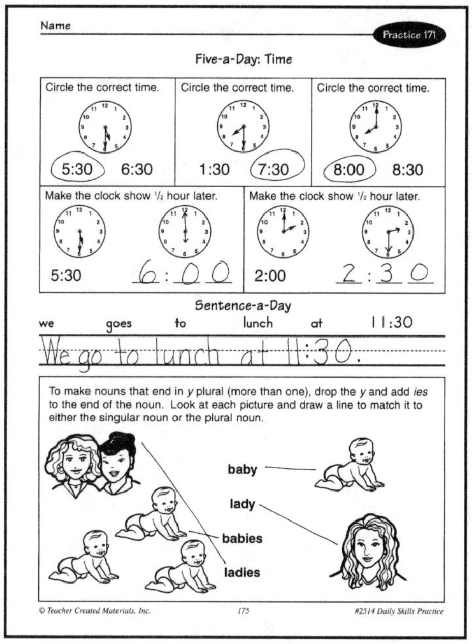

Name Practice 171

Five-a-Day: Time

Circle the correct time.	Circle the correct time.	Circle the correct time.
5:30 6:30	1:30 7:30	8:00 8:30

Make the clock show 1/2 hour later.	Make the clock show 1/2 hour later.
5:30 6:00	2:00 2:30

Sentence-a-Day

we goes to lunch at 11:30

We go to lunch at 11:30.

To make nouns that end in *y* plural (more than one), drop the *y* and add *ies* to the end of the noun. Look at each picture and draw a line to match it to either the singular noun or the plural noun.

baby

lady

babies

ladies

© Teacher Created Materials, Inc. 175 #2514 Daily Skills Practice

Page 176

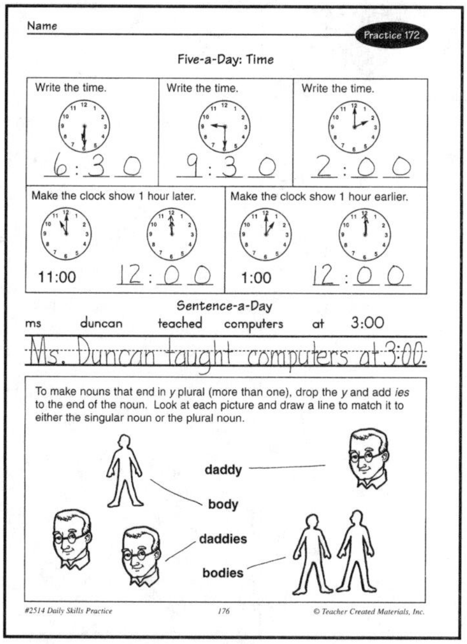

Name Practice 172

Five-a-Day: Time

Write the time.	Write the time.	Write the time.
6:30	9:30	2:00

Make the clock show 1 hour later.	Make the clock show 1 hour earlier.
11:00 12:00	1:00 12:00

Sentence-a-Day

ms duncan teached computers at 3:00

Ms. Duncan taught computers at 3:00.

To make nouns that end in *y* plural (more than one), drop the *y* and add *ies* to the end of the noun. Look at each picture and draw a line to match it to either the singular noun or the plural noun.

daddy

body

daddies

bodies

#2514 Daily Skills Practice 176 © Teacher Created Materials, Inc.

Page 177

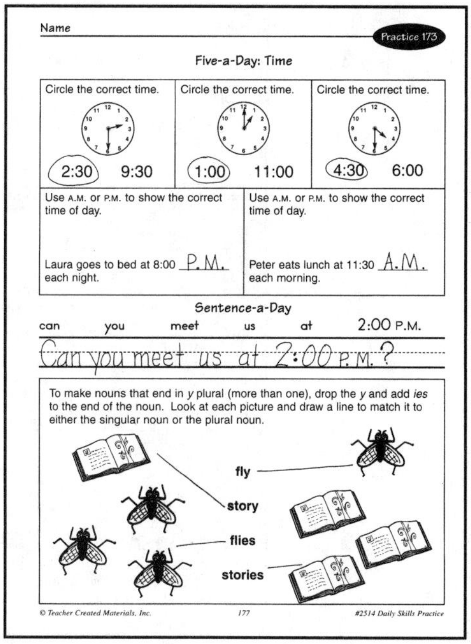

Name Practice 173

Five-a-Day: Time

Circle the correct time.	Circle the correct time.	Circle the correct time.
2:30 9:30	1:00 11:00	4:30 6:00

Use A.M. or P.M. to show the correct time of day.	Use A.M. or P.M. to show the correct time of day.
Laura goes to bed at 8:00 P.M. each night.	Peter eats lunch at 11:30 A.M. each morning.

Sentence-a-Day

can you meet us at 2:00 P.M.

Can you meet us at 2:00 P.M.?

To make nouns that end in *y* plural (more than one), drop the *y* and add *ies* to the end of the noun. Look at each picture and draw a line to match it to either the singular noun or the plural noun.

fly

story

flies

stories

© Teacher Created Materials, Inc. 177 #2514 Daily Skills Practice

Page 178

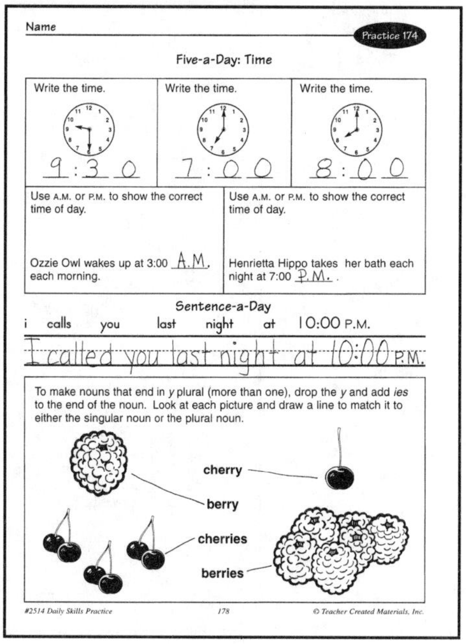

Name Practice 174

Five-a-Day: Time

Write the time.	Write the time.	Write the time.
9:30	7:00	8:00

Use A.M. or P.M. to show the correct time of day.	Use A.M. or P.M. to show the correct time of day.
Ozzie Owl wakes up at 3:00 A.M. each morning.	Henrietta Hippo takes her bath each night at 7:00 P.M. .

Sentence-a-Day

i calls you last night at 10:00 P.M.

I called you last night at 10:00 P.M.

To make nouns that end in *y* plural (more than one), drop the *y* and add *ies* to the end of the noun. Look at each picture and draw a line to match it to either the singular noun or the plural noun.

cherry

berry

cherries

berries

#2514 Daily Skills Practice 178 © Teacher Created Materials, Inc.

Page 179

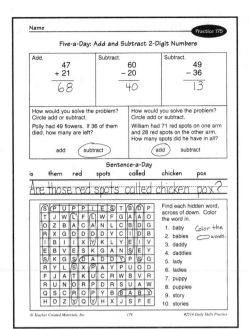

Five-a-Day: Add and Subtract 2-Digit Numbers

Add.	Subtract.	Subtract.
47 + 21 = 68	60 − 20 = 40	49 − 36 = 13

How would you solve the problem? Circle add or subtract.
Polly had 49 flowers. If 36 of them died, how many are left? add (subtract)

How would you solve the problem? Circle add or subtract.
William had 71 red spots on one arm and 28 red spots on the other arm. How many spots did he have in all? (add) subtract

Sentence-a-Day

is them red spots called chicken pox

Are those red spots called chicken pox?

Find each hidden word, across of down. Color the word in.
1. baby
2. babies Color the words.
3. daddy
4. daddies
5. lady
6. ladies
7. puppy
8. puppies
9. story
10. stories

© Teacher Created Materials, Inc. 179 #2514 Daily Skills Practice

---

Page 180

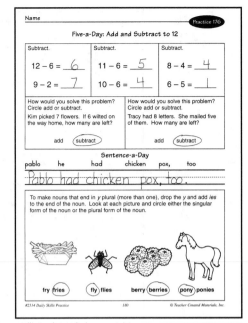

Five-a-Day: Add and Subtract to 12

Subtract.	Subtract.	Subtract.
12 − 6 = 6	11 − 6 = 5	8 − 4 = 4
9 − 2 = 7	10 − 6 = 4	6 − 5 = 1

How would you solve this problem? Circle add or subtract.
Kim picked 7 flowers. If 6 wilted on the way home, how many are left? add (subtract)

How would you solve this problem? Circle add or subtract.
Tracy had 8 letters. She mailed five of them. How many are left? add (subtract)

Sentence-a-Day

pablo he had chicken pox, too

Pablo had chicken pox, too.

To make nouns that end in y plural (more than one), drop the y and add ies to the end of the noun. Look at each picture and circle either the singular form of the noun or the plural form of the noun.

fry (fries)   fly flies   berry (berries)   pony ponies

#2514 Daily Skills Practice 180 © Teacher Created Materials, Inc.

Page 181

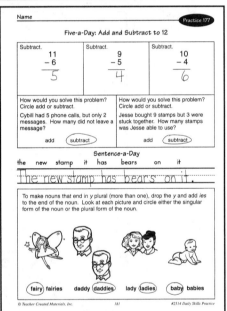

Five-a-Day: Add and Subtract to 12

Subtract.	Subtract.	Subtract.
11 − 6 = 5	9 − 5 = 4	10 − 4 = 6

How would you solve this problem? Circle add or subtract.
Cybill had 5 phone calls, but only 2 messages. How many did not leave a message? add (subtract)

How would you solve this problem? Circle add or subtract.
Jesse bought 9 stamps but 3 were stuck together. How many stamps was Jesse able to use? add (subtract)

Sentence-a-Day

the new stamp it has bears on it

The new stamp has bears on it.

To make nouns that end in y plural (more than one), drop the y and add ies to the end of the noun. Look at each picture and circle either the singular form of the noun or the plural form of the noun.

fairy (fairies)   daddy (daddies)   lady (ladies)   baby babies

© Teacher Created Materials, Inc. 181 #2514 Daily Skills Practice

---

Page 182

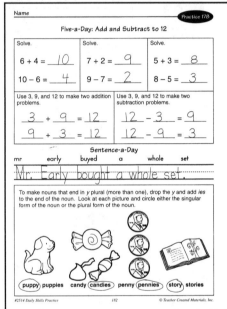

Five-a-Day: Add and Subtract to 12

Solve.	Solve.	Solve.
6 + 4 = 10	7 + 2 = 9	5 + 3 = 8
10 − 6 = 4	9 − 7 = 2	8 − 5 = 3

Use 3, 9, and 12 to make two addition problems.
3 + 9 = 12
9 + 3 = 12

Use 3, 9, and 12 to make two subtraction problems.
12 − 3 = 9
12 − 9 = 3

Sentence-a-Day

mr early buyed a whole set

Mr. Early bought a whole set.

To make nouns that end in y plural (more than one), drop the y and add ies to the end of the noun. Look at each picture and circle either the singular form of the noun or the plural form of the noun.

(puppy) puppies   candy (candies)   penny (pennies)   (story) stories

#2514 Daily Skills Practice 182 © Teacher Created Materials, Inc.

Page 183

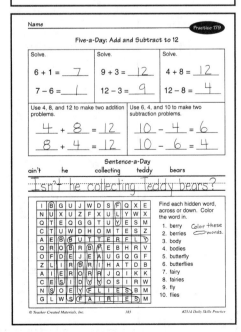

Five-a-Day: Add and Subtract to 12

Solve.	Solve.	Solve.
6 + 1 = 7	9 + 3 = 12	4 + 8 = 12
7 − 6 = 1	12 − 3 = 9	12 − 8 = 4

Use 4, 8, and 12 to make two addition problems.
4 + 8 = 12
8 + 4 = 12

Use 6, 4, and 10 to make two subtraction problems.
10 − 4 = 6
10 − 6 = 4

Sentence-a-Day

ain't he collecting teddy bears

Isn't he collecting Teddy bears?

Find each hidden word, across or down. Color the word in.
1. berry Color these words.
2. berries
3. body
4. bodies
5. butterfly
6. butterflies
7. fairy
8. fairies
9. fly
10. flies

© Teacher Created Materials, Inc. 183 #2514 Daily Skills Practice

---

Page 184

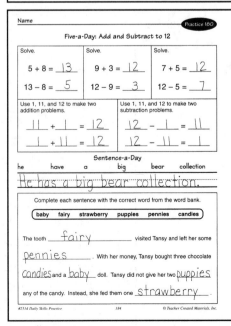

Five-a-Day: Add and Subtract to 12

Solve.	Solve.	Solve.
5 + 8 = 13	9 + 3 = 12	7 + 5 = 12
13 − 8 = 5	12 − 9 = 3	12 − 5 = 7

Use 1, 11, and 12 to make two addition problems.
11 + 1 = 12
1 + 11 = 12

Use 1, 11, and 12 to make two subtraction problems.
12 − 1 = 11
12 − 11 = 1

Sentence-a-Day

he have a big bear collection

He has a big bear collection.

Complete each sentence with the correct word from the word bank.

| baby   fairy   strawberry   puppies   pennies   candies |

The tooth __fairy__ visited Tansy and left her some __pennies__. With her money, Tansy bought three chocolate __candies__ and a __baby__ doll. Tansy did not give her two __puppies__ any of the candy. Instead, she fed them one __strawberry__

#2514 Daily Skills Practice 184 © Teacher Created Materials, Inc.

Page 185

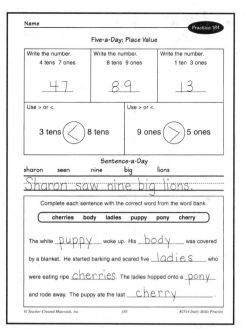

Practice 181

Five-a-Day: Place Value

Write the number. 4 tens 7 ones	Write the number. 8 tens 9 ones	Write the number. 1 ten 3 ones
47	89	13

Use > or <.

3 tens < 8 tens   9 ones > 5 ones

Sentence-a-Day

sharon   seen   nine   big   lions

Sharon saw nine big lions.

Complete each sentence with the correct word from the word bank.

cherries   body   ladies   puppy   pony   cherry

The white puppy woke up. His body was covered by a blanket. He started barking and scared five ladies who were eating ripe cherries. The ladies hopped onto a pony and rode away. The puppy ate the last cherry .

© Teacher Created Materials, Inc.   185   #2514 Daily Skills Practice

---

Page 186

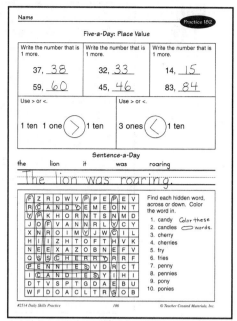

Practice 182

Five-a-Day: Place Value

Write the number that is 1 more.	Write the number that is 1 more.	Write the number that is 1 more.
37, 38	32, 33	14, 15
59, 60	45, 46	83, 84

Use > or <.

1 ten 1 one > 1 ten   3 ones < 1 ten

Sentence-a-Day

the   lion   it   was   roaring

The lion was roaring.

Find each hidden word, across or down. Color the word in.

1. candy   Color these
2. candies   words.
3. cherry
4. cherries
5. fry
6. fries
7. penny
8. pennies
9. pony
10. ponies

#2514 Daily Skills Practice   186   © Teacher Created Materials, Inc.

Page 187

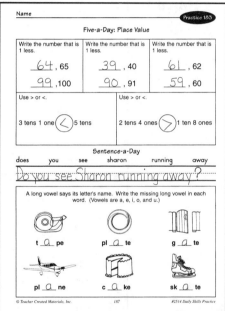

Practice 183

Five-a-Day: Place Value

Write the number that is 1 less.	Write the number that is 1 less.	Write the number that is 1 less.
64, 65	39, 40	61, 62
99, 100	90, 91	59, 60

Use > or <.

3 tens 1 one < 5 tens   2 tens 4 ones > 1 ten 8 ones

Sentence-a-Day

does   you   see   sharon   running   away

Do you see Sharon running away?

A long vowel says its letter's name. Write the missing long vowel in each word. (Vowels are a, e, i, o, and u.)

t a pe   pl a te   g a te

pl a ne   c a ke   sk a te

© Teacher Created Materials, Inc.   187   #2514 Daily Skills Practice

---

Page 188

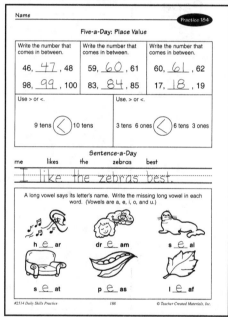

Practice 184

Five-a-Day: Place Value

Write the number that comes in between.	Write the number that comes in between.	Write the number that comes in between.
46, 47, 48	59, 60, 61	60, 61, 62
98, 99, 100	83, 84, 85	17, 18, 19

Use > or <.

9 tens < 10 tens   3 tens 6 ones < 6 tens 3 ones

Sentence-a-Day

me   likes   the   zebras   best

I like the zebras best.

A long vowel says its letter's name. Write the missing long vowel in each word. (Vowels are a, e, i, o, and u.)

h e ar   dr e am   s e al

s e at   p e as   l e af

#2514 Daily Skills Practice   188   © Teacher Created Materials, Inc.

Page 189

Practice 185

Five-a-Day: Place Value

Write even or odd.	Write even or odd.	Write even or odd.
22, 24, 26, 28	41, 43, 45, 47	65, 67, 69, 71
even	odd	odd

Mystery Number: I am an even number. I am greater than 30 and less than 50. When you count by 10's you say my name. What number am I?

The mystery number is 40 .

Mystery Number: I am an odd number. I am greater than 80 and less than 90. When you count by 5's you say my name. What number am I?

The mystery number is 85 .

Sentence-a-Day

which   animal   does   karen   like   best

Which animal does Karen like best?

A long vowel says its letter's name. Write the missing long vowel in each word. (Vowels are a, e, i, o, and u.)

pr i ze   m i ce   b i ke

h i ve   r i ce   l i me

© Teacher Created Materials, Inc.   189   #2514 Daily Skills Practice

---

Page 190

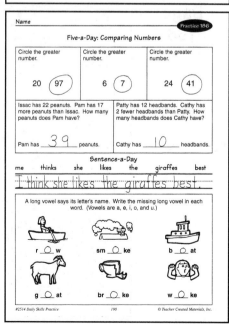

Practice 186

Five-a-Day: Comparing Numbers

Circle the greater number.	Circle the greater number.	Circle the greater number.
20 (97)	6 (7)	24 (41)

Issac has 22 peanuts. Pam has 17 more peanuts than Issac. How many peanuts does Pam have?

Pam has 39 peanuts.

Patty has 12 headbands. Cathy has 2 fewer headbands than Patty. How many headbands does Cathy have?

Cathy has 10 headbands.

Sentence-a-Day

me   thinks   she   likes   the   giraffes   best

I think she likes the giraffes best.

A long vowel says its letter's name. Write the missing long vowel in each word. (Vowels are a, e, i, o, and u.)

r o w   sm o ke   b o at

g o at   br o ke   w o ke

#2514 Daily Skills Practice   190   © Teacher Created Materials, Inc.

Page 191

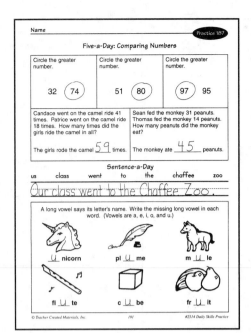

Page 192

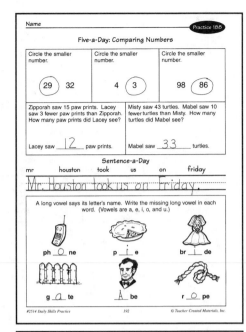

Page 193

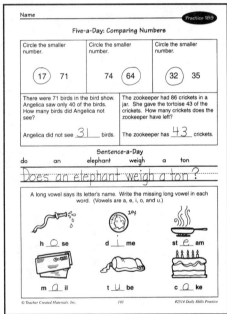

Page 194

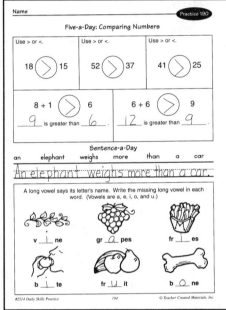

Page 195

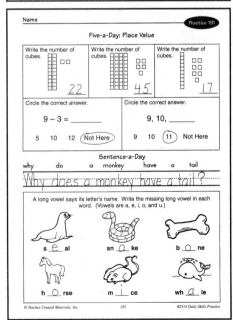

Page 196

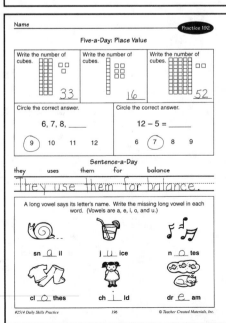

Page 197

Name

Practice 193

Five-a-Day: Place Value

Draw the number of tens and ones needed in cubes to make 21.	Draw the number of tens and ones needed in cubes to make 33.	Draw the number of tens and ones needed in cubes to make 18.

Circle the correct answer.	Circle the correct answer.
5 + 6 = ____	10 + 2 = ____
6 (11) 12 Not here	9 11 13 (Not here)

Sentence-a-Day

we're   gonna   watch   the   seal   swim

We're going to watch the seal swim.

Read the scrambled sentence. Write the words in the correct order.

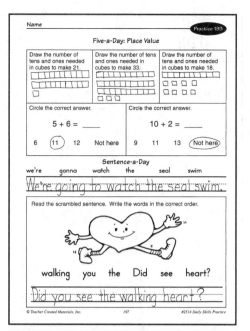

walking   you   the   Did   see   heart?

Did you see the walking heart?

© Teacher Created Materials, Inc.   197   #2514 Daily Skills Practice

---

Page 198

Name

Practice 194

Five-a-Day: Place Value

Draw the number of tens and ones needed in cubes to make 9.	Draw the number of tens and ones needed in cubes to make 25.	Draw the number of tens and ones needed in cubes to make 40.

Draw the hands to show the correct time. The camel rides begin at 10:00 A.M.	Draw the hands to show the correct time. The bird show is over at 11:30 A.M.

Sentence-a-Day

me   and   india   liked   the   rhino   the   best

India and I liked the rhino the best.

Write the correct blend at the end of each word.

st   nd   nd   st

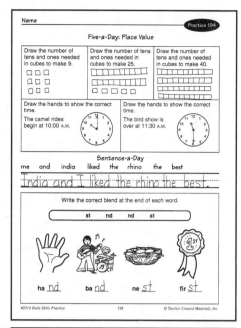

ha nd   ba nd   ne st   fir st

#2514 Daily Skills Practice   198   © Teacher Created Materials, Inc.

Page 199

Name

Practice 195

Five-a-Day: Place Value

Draw the number of tens and ones needed in cubes to make 37.	Draw the number of tens and ones needed in cubes to make 12.	Draw the number of tens and ones needed in cubes to make 54.

Draw the hands to show the correct time. The zookeeper feeds the snakes at 2:00 P.M.	Draw the hands to show the correct time. The bison goes for a walk at 5:00 P.M.

Sentence-a-Day

can   us   go   to   the   zoo   again

Can we go to the zoo again?

Write the correct blend at the end of each word.

nt   rm   rt   st

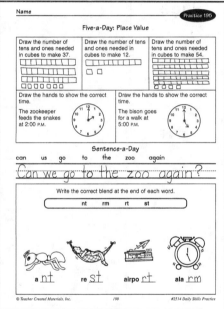

a nt   re st   airpo rt   ala rm

© Teacher Created Materials, Inc.   199   #2514 Daily Skills Practice

---

Page 200

Name

Practice 196

Five-a-Day: Addition Facts to 18

Add.	Add.	Add.
7 + 4 = 11	9 + 5 = 14	7 + 9 = 16
4 + 9 = 13	8 + 7 = 15	7 + 6 = 13

Jenny made 8 kites. Tammy made 6 kites. How many kites did they make in all?	Chester saw 6 clouds that looked like lions and 9 clouds that looked like tigers. How many clouds did Chester see in all?
They made 14 kites in all.	Chester saw 15 clouds in all.

Sentence-a-Day

the   wind   are   blowing   hard   today

The wind is blowing hard today.

Write the correct blend at the end of each word.

ng   nk   nt   rn

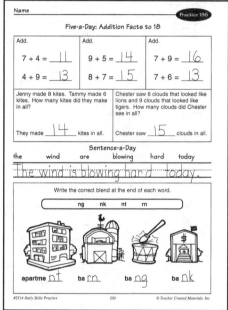

apartme nt   ba rn   ba ng   ba nk

#2514 Daily Skills Practice   200   © Teacher Created Materials, Inc.

Page 201

Name

Practice 197

Five-a-Day: Addition Facts to 18

Solve.	Solve.	Solve.
6 + 8 = 14	4 + 9 = 13	6 + 9 = 15
8 + 7 = 15	6 + 8 = 14	5 + 8 = 13

I have 13 books from my brother and sister. My sister gave me 7 of the books. How many did my brother give me?	Dad has 12 kites. If 7 of them are box kites, how many are not box kites?
My brother gave me 6 books.	5 are not box kites.

Sentence-a-Day

its   too   windy   to   fly   a   kite

It's too windy to fly a kite.

Write the correct blend at the end of each word.

lt   mp   rd   rd

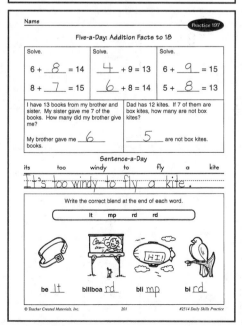

be lt   billboa rd   bli mp   bi rd

© Teacher Created Materials, Inc.   201   #2514 Daily Skills Practice

---

Page 202

Name

Practice 198

Five-a-Day: Addition Facts to 18

Add.	Add.	Add.
9 + 9 = 18	8 + 8 = 16	7 + 9 = 16
4 + 8 = 12	9 + 3 = 12	13 + 0 = 13

There were 9 dandelions in Terri's front yard and 7 in her backyard. How many dandelions were there in all?	Doug collects flowers. He has 5 roses and 9 wildflowers in his collection. How many flowers does Doug have in all?
There were 16 dandelions in all.	Doug has 14 flowers in all.

Sentence-a-Day

plants   needs   soil,   water,   and   sunlight

Plants need soil, water, and sunlight.

Write the correct blend at the end of each word.

ld   mp   rd   st

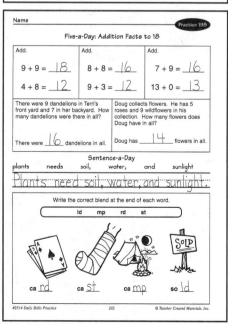

ca rd   ca st   camp mp   so ld

#2514 Daily Skills Practice   202   © Teacher Created Materials, Inc.

Page 203

Practice 199

Five-a-Day: Addition Facts to 18

Add.

3 + 3 + 4 = 10
6 + 3 + 3 = 12

Add.

2 + 2 + 6 = 10
4 + 4 + 4 = 12

Add.

6 + 2 + 4 = 12
3 + 3 + 6 = 12

Rosita had 5 yellow pencils, 1 pink pencil, and 2 green pencils. How many pencils did she have in all?

Rosita had 8 pencils in all.

Luke had 4 baseball gloves, 5 bats, and 4 uniforms. How many pieces of baseball equipment did Luke have in all?

Luke had 13 pieces in all.

Sentence-a-Day

are   a   cactus   prickly

Is a cactus prickly ?

Write the correct blend at the end of each word.

mp   rk   rn   st

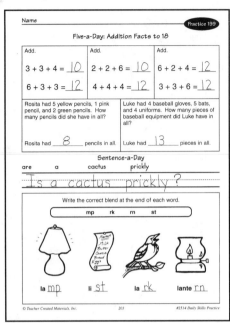

la mp   li st   la rk   lante rn

© Teacher Created Materials, Inc.   203   #2514 Daily Skills Practice

---

Page 204

Practice 200

Five-a-Day: Addition Facts to 18

Add.

1 + 4 + 5 = 10
2 + 6 + 2 = 10

Add.

5 + 4 + 5 = 14
6 + 3 + 2 = 11

Add.

2 + 5 + 3 = 10
4 + 3 + 3 = 10

Penny has 2 red rings, 7 green rings, and 1 white ring. How many rings does Penny have in all?

Penny has 10 rings in all.

Christopher has 5 pennies, 2 nickels, and 7 dimes. How many coins does he have in all?

Christopher has 14 coins in all.

Sentence-a-Day

cactuses   grows   in   the   hot   desert

Cactuses grow in the hot desert.

Write the correct blend at the end of each word.

ng   rd   sk   st

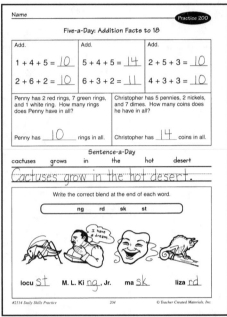

locu st   M. L. Ki ng , Jr.   ma sk   liza rd

#2514 Daily Skills Practice   204   © Teacher Created Materials, Inc.

Page 205

Practice 201

Five-a-Day: Subtraction Facts to 18

Subtract.

13 − 4 = 9
15 − 7 = 8

Subtract.

14 − 6 = 8
13 − 5 = 8

Subtract.

15 − 8 = 7
14 − 9 = 5

Trevor saw 13 cactuses. If 8 of them had flowers, how many cactuses did not have flowers?

5 cactuses did not have flowers.

Dennis earned 14 game points. He needs 18 points to win. How many more points must he earn to win?

He must earn 4 more points.

Sentence-a-Day

bees   makes   honey   from   nectar

Bees make honey from nectar.

Write the correct blend at the end of each word.

nt   nt   rt   rt

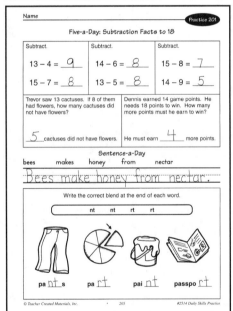

pa nt s   pa rt   pai nt   passpo rt

© Teacher Created Materials, Inc.   205   #2514 Daily Skills Practice

---

Page 206

Practice 202

Five-a-Day: Add and Subtract to 18

Solve.

15 − 9 = 6
13 − 6 = 7

Solve.

12 + 3 = 15
13 − 9 = 4

Solve.

15 − 6 = 9
13 + 5 = 18

There were 13 aphids on Lucas' roses. He brushed 8 of them off. How many aphids were left?

There were 5 aphids left.

Jonas planted 18 flowers in his yard. The grasshoppers ate 9 of them. How many flowers does Jonas have left?

Jonas has 9 flowers left.

Sentence-a-Day

what   does   ladybugs   like   to   eat

What do ladybugs like to eat ?

Write the correct digraph at the end of each word.

ch   sh   sh   th

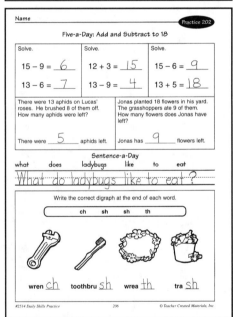

wren ch   toothbru sh   wrea th   tra sh

#2514 Daily Skills Practice   206   © Teacher Created Materials, Inc.
